Woman in Levi's

Illustrated by VIC DONAHUE

Woman in Levi's

EULALIA BOURNE

THE UNIVERSITY OF ARIZONA PRESS

LEVI'S is a
registered trademark
of Levi Strauss & Co.
San Francisco, California

Fourth printing 1972
Third printing 1968
Second printing 1967
First printing 1967

THE UNIVERSITY OF ARIZONA PRESS

I.S.B.N. 0–8165–0103–3 (cl)
L.C. No. 66–27382

CONTENTS

Acknowledgments

MY INDEBTEDNESS IS GREAT to the friends, neighbors, and relatives whose aid and comfort assured the survival of the GF Bar Ranch. Foremost come my three "pardners," octogenarians all before death ended our association. Soon after I moved from Pepper Sauce Canyon in the Santa Catalina Mountains to the foothill roughs of the Galiuros on the rim of the San Pedro River valley, someone in Mammoth summed up the news:

"I hear a schoolteacher and three old men have moved up to the Hendrickson Place."

These were the three: James W. Martin (the Uncle) spent his last eighteen years and would have spent his last dollar for the benefit of this little ranch. Juan Espinosa, "Juanón" (called in this book the Old Vaquero), helped to keep us in business with both courage and cowmanship. Calvert Coates, the Star Boarder, a retired mining engineer, London-born, does not figure often only because it is the story of a working hard-scrabble ranch, and no matter how the rest of us strained and sweated, he remained the English gentleman. At his retirement, he came to the ranch because he liked my cooking and wanted to be outdoors. He stayed seventeen years; but he did not dress like a rancher, or speak like a rancher, or act like a rancher. He knew nothing about working cattle and did not try to learn. His contributions were keeping the roads passable and carrying off the garbage. He made his own schedules and worked alone. If one of the others went out to help him cut brush or lift rocks, he quit. In his relations with the Uncle and the Old Vaquero he was a segregationist. It was years before he understood why I kept them around. One night as we sat by the fire (in winter time he waited up for me and kept the cabin warm) he said, with an air of discovery: "Old Jim is an outdoor man. He mends the fences and takes care of the corrals." He knew that Juan rode horseback everyday, but he had only a vague idea why. He knew no Spanish and the little English the Old Vaquero understood did not include a British accent.

The three were all loners, and there was no brotherly love among them. The magnetic hoop that held them together in the lonely little far-off shack on Pepper Sauce was the woman who drove home from schoolteaching on Friday nights. That was the day they shaved and cleaned up. They said even the dogs knew when it was Friday and sat out on the edge of the canyon wall waiting. When I got out to open the gate nearly a mile below the house I could hear them barking and I knew they could hear my car.

Juanón had been a family man in his youth. After his wife died he maintained a home for their three little girls. He said he had been tempted to marry again two or three times, but he could not bear to inflict a stepmother on his little ones. They were grownups when he came to the GF Bar. He remained devoted to them, spent his holidays with them, and gave them what money he had. But he would not live with them, he said, because they had married scoundrels who abused them and he would not see his daughters suffer.

Since he was twelve years old (when his father died) Uncle Jim had taken care of his mother and older sisters.

He still had his two elderly, almost helpless sisters in his house in the village of Oracle when he came to live at the ranch. To the last, he had a brave man's weakness for dogs and women, and his devotion was completely unselfish.

Never having had a dependent, Cal's worry had been for Number One only. The two others preceded him a few years on the ranch, but for a time he considered it his duty to observe them closely during the week and report their shortcomings to me. "Old Jim," he said, "is a wasteful cook. He uses too much shortening in his biscuits. Expensive vegetable shortening. You should get cheap lard for the men."

"I think the vegetable shortening is better for their health." (Cal did not eat the biscuits. He ate bakery bread.)

"But he feeds them to the dogs!"

"Well, if he runs out of dogfeed he has to feed them something!"

Cal forgave my folly, and in his way never ceased trying to help me. The others could not see why they had to put up with him, but they, too, overlooked my folly. These three, with my dogs and cats, made up my menage. They were more than family. They were friends.

Four "daughters" who helped during their university weekends and vacations, and whose interest has continued since they married and started families, should not go unnamed. They were Caroline, Mrs. John McMakin, Casa Grande, Arizona; Doris, Mrs. Tom McCord, Lafayette, California; Shirley, Mrs. Charles Tribolet, and Lois, Mrs. Harold Hamer, both of Tucson, Arizona. We had nicknames for them and loved them for their precious friendship. They seldom came all at the same time. When that happened they brought young men with them and there was general bedlam getting enough saddlehorses and tack and sufficient groceries and cold drinks and bedrolls. Usually Doris (we called her "Buck") had to ride bareback and she was the gal who could do it, eight or ten miles without a break. Once I scolded her for spooking a sore-eyed calf I was trying to corral. She jumped on her little pacing mare bareback, she herself barelegged and barefooted, and dashed off through rocks and cactus after him. In about an hour, to my astonishment — no real cowboy could have done it — she brought him back. The West lost a great horsewoman when our Buck married an indoor man (C.P.A.) and became a library assistant.

Caroline, whom the Uncle named "Sweetheart," was a frail midwesterner Buck brought out for a week one summer. I was afraid the ranch would be too rough for her. But she liked it so much she never ceased coming back. She was a wonderful morale-builder, attentive to the old men, kind to me when I blew up from fatigue and frustration.

Shirley and Lois (we called them "Buzz" and "Cinco" and they are still so called), attractive, ambitious young women, cared little for the outdoor life. Their interest was in Buck, Sweetheart, and me. They took an apartment in Tucson and Caroline went to live with them at the end of the term. All got jobs except Cinco who became a city teacher. They had money to spend and entertained me lavishly on Friday evenings when school started.

Among the boys from my school who at times volunteered to go home with me holidays and weekends and do ranch chores for the fun of it were Frank and Dave McGee, Joe and Denny Nolan, Paul and Richard McGee, and Lynn Harris, all from Sierrita School; and, in earlier years from another school, Frank, Pancho, Arturo, and Victor Aros; and Trini Padilla.

It has been my privilege to be chosen "grandmother"

by two boys who have helped me very much over the years. Dave McGee has stayed with me more than anybody after the three old ones died. He was my pupil through all the elementary grades and never gave me an unpleasant moment. He liked to help, and he was good help. He built roads, fixed fences, laid pipelines, burned chollas, and helped with the cows. In this last he was exceptional because he would take my directions. When I said, "Wait here at the forks of the canyon while I ride the south ridges; and hold anything that I flush out," he stayed right there no matter how long I was gone or whether any cattle showed up or not. He is now a family man in business for himself, but when I face a crisis, he is my boy!

Preston Boan, now a professional horse trainer, fell in love with my old saddlehorses as a nine-year-old. When he lived two miles up the creek one year he came down almost every day to see the horses, feed them, touch them, and eventually to ride them. When he stayed with me during school vacations, together we got a surprising amount of work done. He is still the one to take over when I break a leg.

A role I have been happy to accept is that of "aunt" to some young men who have helped me in their spare time. The first was Wilbur Minderman. When I was alone, before Uncle Jim and Big Juan came, I was losing cattle alarmingly. Wilbur, then working in a store six days a week, ten hours a day, had ranch in his blood and pity in his heart. He came out and rode for me every Sunday, all day. I insisted on paying him. Two dollars a day!

Years later, after Uncle Jim died and Old Juan was crippled with arthritis, I couldn't brand my big spring calves. One November day I came upon a little bunch of cows with four long-ears with them at the spring in Prospect Canyon. Billy, the little bay horse, and I got them home and corraled. Then I went for help. I thought Camille Pierson, an outdoor woman who had been my neighbor on Pepper Sauce, could help me throw and tie down the big calves. But she had gone hunting. All the local cowboys, real and facsimile, were on roundups. I went into Roy's Place and asked if old Berry was available. He was not a cowboy; he was a fellow who had done some plumbing for me. But he was manpower.

"He was here last night," said Roy.

"Was he sober?"

"No."

I glanced down the long bar where three young men and two young women sat looking at me.

"Anyone here want to go to the ranch and help me brand four big calves?" I asked, laughing at myself.

"Yes!" they said. They were getting ready to go on a picnic. Why not the ranch? They picked up their grocery box and six-packs and followed. Their leader was Donn Haines who appears in this chronicle as The Nephew. He had lived on a ranch as a small boy, and readily took to this place as home, driving back and forth each day to his job at the mine fifteen miles away. He stayed three years, leaving a big gap when he sold his cattle and went back to college.

One summer he brought out "Hoppy" (William W. Hopkins, now a journalist in Anchorage, Alaska), a university student who worked in the mine during vacations. Hoppy was the one to encourage me about my manuscripts. I am indebted to him for my nice flagpole, too.

Not long after they left, their place was taken by Bill (William F.) Brown, the best-liked man in all this countryside. He also had spent his boyhood on a ranch. When he heard I was alone he came to offer his help. It was good help. He had an exacting job, a big family, and, unknown to us at the time, a fatal illness; but he gathered this needy outfit under his wing. He shod the horses, gathered the yearlings, and helped with the pump and the hauling and all the hard jobs. I never felt whipped by adversities when Bill was on call ten miles away. He is gone now. This place will never be the same.

Nor could anyone take the place of Pete Carey, my present helper. For a long time now he has been the mainstay of the outfit. Pete is a security guard at the non-working mine two miles up the canyon. A man of action who cannot bear to be idle, when there is nothing for him to do at the mine, he comes down here, grabs a shovel, pick or axe and makes the work fly. He is here each morning and evening, since Cal and Bill died, to check on me and to help with the chores. A proud man, he will not accept cash from a "pore ole widderwoman," but only an occasional gift of shirt or sweater and a cooked meal. Pete says he would go crazy up at the mine, but "there's always something to do at the ranch," and that's an understatement for sure.

My own relatives long ago moved out of Arizona, beyond my reach. The two sisters who liked the ranch and loved animals and came so many times to help me, Bessie Primrose and Ruby Drorbaugh, are no longer living. I now express deep gratitude to my loyal, long-suffering younger sisters who live in California, Sabrey (Mrs. Claude) Botkin and Bernice (Mrs. Carl) Richard; to my nieces Bernice (Martha) Goodwin, Liz Hackelman, and Virginia Rice; and to my nephews Louis Collins, Collins Hath, and Clarence and Roll Drorbaugh, for their patience and affection.

Very special thanks are extended to Abbie Keith, secretary to the Arizona Cattle Growers Association for half a lifetime; to Joyce Mercer, my benevolent neighbor; and to Faye McGee, my sympathetic "fairy goddaughter," for their encouragement in writing this book.

And to the memory of two great University of Arizona English professors who taught me — Frances Perry and Allegra Frazier — I am profoundly grateful.

Woman in Levi's

CHAPTER 1

Kids and Cows

Thirty years and more in the San Pedro Valley have not lessened my sense of awe, as I return from a trip outside to crest the western rim and see the grandeur and color of thousands of square miles spread out before me. I had been an Arizona resident for a quarter of a century before I learned that the state has *two* scenic wonders carved out over millions of years by great river systems: the Grand Canyon of the Colorado, and the San Pedro River Valley which was named for St. Peter by the padres and conquistadores who passed this way in 1540, eighty years before the Pilgrims landed. The Grand Canyon is out of this world. But the San Pedro Valley, although far from crowded, is peopled. For the most part its denizens are earthy ones, wresting their living from the ground, in some cases for four or five generations: farmers, ranchers, miners.

I came into it (sent sight unseen by the county school superintendent at Tucson) to teach a small accommodation school at Redington, about halfway the hundred-mile length of the river — the only one of consequence in the United States that flows north in its entirety. Redington School was the most remote in Pima County. It was seventy-five miles from Tucson, mostly over rough, two-wheel unkept roads that literally disappeared when it rained.

1

The isolation and limited enrollment were appealing. I had overworked audaciously for years while teaching non-readers in overcrowded rooms and earning a university degree simultaneously. Moreover, I had suffered severe emotional damage in my personal life. I wanted to hide far-off by myself to lick my wounds and have a go at writing. I would do my duty by the handful of little ranchers for the minimum hours a day, then uncover my portable and whack away at my creations secure from interruptions and the cares of the world. Then I met my pupils.

One fateful September morning I put on a new blue dress, walked the two hundred yards up the mesa to the little time-washed adobe school shack on a bench overlooking the river road and the wooded bottom land, and changed the whole course of my life. From that day forward I was hooked — not only by the little cowpunchers, but by their enchanting environment.

Those Redington kids were the biggest school challenge I ever had. There were seven boys and four girls that first year; the most advanced two were supposed to be in the fourth grade but they stumbled over simple words like *yes* and *you*. Nobody in the room could read, but all wanted to. They knew that they did not know the traditional subject matter common to their grades, and they wanted to do something about it. All but the two Anglos — second and third graders — had a language handicap (and in a way these also did) but they made it plain they wanted to overcome it. And they were the friendliest, most affectionate, most anxious-to-please children I ever met. As a group they had never saluted the flag, memorized a poem, had a book read to them, listened to music in the schoolroom, given a community entertainment, or gone on a school expedition to the outside world. The big world

was only over the mountains. But for most of the Redington kids it might as well have been over the Pacific Ocean.
The year before, their teacher had been an unhappy girl
right out of the university with a degree in domestic
science who was marking time until she could teach in
high school. She was nice to the children and probably
thought she was doing them a favor to promote them. Red-
faced little Ike, statistically in the second grade, couldn't
write his name or read a pre-primer. He said timidly: "The
teacher never teached me nothing."

Did I have fun!

Within a few days the kids and I were hitting it off just
fine, and the whole community opened its arms. I was
oversupplied with fresh corn, string beans, and squashes;
morning and night I received a bottle of milk delivered
to my door by tiny hands of adorable pre-school little girls.
A horse and saddle were placed at my disposal. Everywhere I was met by glad smiles. From dismissal time until
dark as I rode with the school children or the cowboys,
up and down the river bottom I heard happy young ones
singing the songs and singing-games I had taught them.
Evenings I uncovered the little typewriter. I worked at it
until bedtime: making lesson plans, individual worksheets,
and daily lesson tests. The hours at school were so short.
My little cowpunchers had to make up for lost time.

One must not get the impression that I was a city girl
green to all the varying ways of the wilds. I was an exile,
home at last. I was born, on another frontier, on my
father's homestead and do not remember when I first rode
horseback. I do remember a big streak-faced sorrel called
Old Timber that I used to ride; and they tell me I was
only three years old when we moved away. My first teaching job, when I was a teen-ager, was in the Verde Valley
in Yavapai County at a most delightful farming-ranching

place, Beaver Creek. (Strange to say, after more than forty years I now and then get letters from some who were pupils in that school.)

In early childhood and young womanhood cows and horses and what goes with them were integral parts of my existence. The saddest, loneliest years I have known were those when I taught and studied and beat my wings against the containing walls of the city. Redington gave me back freedom and joy and my birthright to space and privacy. It also introduced me to the San Pedro, the untamed, often ferocious river, and encouraged me to take root in its locale, to receive its comforts along with its hardships, its crises with its inspiration; and to give back to the demanding environment such strength, capacity, endurance, and hope as make up a fleeting human life.

It was at the beginning of my third year at Redington that I took the plunge and filed on a homestead, not fully decided that it was for keeps. There was no open land near the school, for the big Carlink Ranch which our school accommodated covered almost the whole valley both sides of the river for about twenty miles.

There is a dot on the map, in the extreme northeast corner of Pima County, marked *Redington*. But if you go looking for the town it isn't there. People "just riding around to see the country" would stop at the school to inquire for a gas station, a cafe, a store. There were none.

"This is only a private ranch," I'd say. "Your next town is Oracle. To reach it you go fourteen miles down the river — which you may not be able to cross when you get to the ford — and thirteen miles up steep slopes and deep canyons to the divide. Or you can go back to Benson, forty-eight miles up the river."

Many of these trippers were disgruntled; some were seriously inconvenienced. They said harsh things about mapmakers. They were right. At the place called Redington, there is only the headquarters of the long-established Carlink Ranch. Except for the Big House and some sheds and storage buildings, when I went there the only other houses were the teacherage, perhaps fifty yards up the slope east of the Big House, and the school farther up on the mesa. Around the bend about a quarter of a mile from the ranch was a private home, one room of which was the postoffice. Rosa, mother of two of my little cowpunchers, was the postmistress. Mail was brought down from Benson three times a week.

A few years before, the place had been in charge of a woman who ran it mainly as a guest ranch. There were over twenty rooms in the Big House. The living room, with its huge fireplace and fifteen-foot ceiling, was like the great hall in a feudal castle.

I asked how the spot got its name. Natives told me that many, many years ago a group of engineers and surveyors camped under the great cottonwood (the biggest I'd ever seen) on the flat below the ranchhouse while laying out a route for a railroad which was to traverse the Valley from Winkelman to Benson. The railroad never materialized. It seems the chief engineer was named Redington. And, to much confusion, his name lingers on.

Looking for a place to settle, I consulted with the neighbors, chief among them the one who appears in these pages as The Old Cowman, and finally decided on a hard-to-get-to spot in Pepper Sauce Canyon, twelve miles from Oracle, five miles above where the River Road crosses the canyon, and twenty-two miles from my school.

In fine weather the journey could be made in a little less than an hour and a half. If it was raining — which meant getting stuck in muddy dips and flats — or if the river was up, I had to drive around the Catalina-Rincon range through Oracle, Tucson, and Benson, a distance of 150 miles! The government was very touchy about a homesteader's being on the land every night and of course my venture began in an exceptionally wet year. The ranchers in the upper Pepper Sauce country, I heard later, resenting me as an intruding nester, were betting I could never stick out the three years required to prove up. They lost. I stayed eighteen years and six months, before moving my whole outfit.

In the beginning I did not know that I was sidling into the cow business. My aim was to have a place to live during no-school months, a place to store my things so that I wouldn't be forever packing and moving. The site was chosen because it had available water. Frank Waters, an old Texas "mudhen" (a fellow who tends wells and windmills and pumps), kindly helped me salvage some pipes from an abandoned mine, open up a shallow well in the bottom of the canyon at the foot of a giant cottonwood, and put in a water system. This he did, at great labor, for sixty dollars a month and his favorite food — "picked-out pecans" — which I took to him weekends with other supplies for his project and his cold wet camp.

One cold day early in December, as soon as there was water up on the sloping shelf above the danger of canyon floods, I pitched a small tent under a beautiful mesquite tree and took possession of one of the last grazing sections Uncle Sam passed out to homeless citizens. The next problem was a cabin. The Old Cowman found some very hungry Mexicans who came out to make adobes and lay the walls. My job was to keep them from freezing or starving to death, for the rain and snow delayed them so much they made nothing on their contract. They burned all the wood in the area trying to dry the adobes. But they did a good job. To this day the walls still stand without a crack.

The Cowman got disgusted because I insisted on fancy stuff — a fireplace and a bathroom. Old Frank stayed with me and he and I did the carpenter work. In five months the one-room house, with bath, was liveable. One Sunday evening in April I made a big fire in the nice big chimney, piled my bedroll on the floor before it and for the first time in my life slept in a home of my very own. The cabin smelled of damp earth and new lumber. It was eight years before I could buy a can of paint. By that time the woodwork had mellowed to such natural beauty that I could not violate it. The white pine floor needed so much scrubbing that in the ninth year I "went for broke" and bought linoleum to cover it.

My Redington friends advised me to go to the land office at Phoenix and apply for some state leased land. I did. And, to my astonishment and the chagrin of my immediate neighbor whose public domain range I had butted into as a nester, I was allotted some leased sections adjacent to my homestead. Old Frank made a good cement *pila* (round drinking trough) on the rise above the house; and I made a stick and wire corral and a sheetiron shed for my horse. The stage was set. Lacking only were the four-footed members of the cast — the cattle.

It was a time when business had been allowed to go its own way — that is, downhill; when no regard was taken for social responsibility in the world of economics; when farm products were unsalable, and livestock was worthless. Nobody had ever heard of controls. War was merely a smudge on the horizon. We river people bumbled along with very little profit. Our standard of living was such that a teacher making a salary of $150 a month was considered a potential employer and a lender of currency. So I bought fifty cows, many of them of good ages, most of them bred, for fifteen dollars apiece. I was in business.

From the day I took delivery on the cows, life has been one grand crisis after another. The neighbor into whose open range (which he had used free of charge for many years, as had his predecessors — for it was government land) I had moved, apparently with the intention to stay, began to take action. He turned out a hundred mares to eat up my grass and drink the water pumped from my well. He hadn't counted on his hostess. I couldn't afford a fence, but I had plenty of strength that summer. Each morning at daylight I saddled Buddy, one of the best cow horses that ever bumped a rock in this rough country, and took after those mares. I ran them so much that it got so my horse didn't have to work up a sweat. As soon as they sighted us atop a ridge, they took off down country, manes and tails flying in the breeze. They had to go all the way to the river — about ten miles — to water and were mixing with the wild horses, so he had to gather them and take them home.

Solutions have not always been so simple. If I make a mistake with my pupils, I can hope their next teacher will rectify it. When I default on a note, the banker can be persuaded to renew it. When I miss on the cattle, it is at once disastrous and often fatal.

With western ranch neighbors, no telling what may happen.

A cowboy of boyish winsomeness, so young he was easily enamored of horses, cattle, the countryside, and a woman's kitchen, took up a homestead five miles down my canyon and called it The Windmill Ranch. In time propinquity took effect and we merged our interests. He could stay to look after the livestock (he had a bunch of horses and mares, and a few head of cattle) and I could go off to school for money to run on. It wasn't such a startling arrangement: since the dawn of history small principalities have been joined by marriage to make more powerful ones.

For three years we fought together against the impossible odds. Then we fought each other. He heard the enticing call of the fast buck; also, there was a female voice in the siren chorus that called to him.

"You want to *have* something," he said. "I want to *make* something."

As they say in England, he shot the moon, although his soft heart grieved at leaving me holding the fort alone. "Sell the goddam place!" he said. But the goddam place was my Baby.

Cattle on their home range are fascinating creatures; and part of their charm — as with children or pets — derives from their constant need for supervision and assistance. Owing to drought, range depletion, pests, and other infirmities and calamities Nature arranges to plague the flesh, there is always something you can do for them.

All kinds of cattle interest me, but I have a special fellow-feeling for cows. They wear themselves out, suffer patiently, fight boldly, and develop shocking tenderness for the young who, usually one at a time, share such a small portion of their lives.

There was old New Mexico. (My cows, like Mrs. Wigg's daughters, have geographical names.) She caused me so much trouble and weariness when she had wooden tongue (a bovine disease about which little is known) and subsequent starvation, and I battled so long to save her, against her will, that I had a notion to quit and knock her in the head. Months later I rode up on her at a remote water hole in the canyon just at dark. She looked good. She was a cow once more instead of a bony caricature. By her side stood a little bull calf, the spitting image of her. She raised her head and looked at me with such pride, such fierce joy in life that I felt the glow of it myself.

In this land of little rain if you own your own water system, you lead with your chin. If you brand your calves in the summer you have to take a chance on losing them to flies and screwworms. If you don't brand them they'll get lost or they will be staggish. If you ride the range every day you neglect your housework and other duties. If you don't ride, some cattle will go blind with pinkeye or otherwise be fouled. Any time you turn your back the pump will break down and you must throw yourself on the mercy of an overworked mechanic miles away who would much rather not bother with you. And overshadowing everything else in this semi-desert is the worry about the uncertainty of rain.

But from the start there were compensations. Some of us are born to like animals that live free in wide uncluttered spaces; to enjoy riding out in the dawn in a crumpled land where the far hills and escarpments are touched with glory by the rising sun. And I had another love — teaching school. To me guiding children to learn was a natural endowment; I never had any training in the courses laid out by professors in charge of teacher's colleges. By the time I entered the university I knew by experience what was taught in education classes in my day. I enrolled in the College of Letters, Arts, and Sciences. I had plenty to learn there.

Purely by chance I found my niche when I went to Redington to become a sort of governess to poverty-touched ranch children. I stayed with the vocation twenty-three rewarding years. Not rewarding, however, in the matter of money. That's where the cows came in. Teaching little cowpunchers and raising cattle are complementary like ham and eggs.

Those first hard summers when I was getting my "boot"

training in cattle growing, after showers — and now and then a rain — had made green feed it was a pleasure to ride among the cows and see them so busy getting fat that they scarcely raised their heads to look at us. We had time to make a barn and some good mesquite corrals and put in a supply of hay. About the time we got the roads repaired from the flood damage it was time to go back to school.

Accommodation schools were emergency measures later wiped out by developing affluence. Now huge yellow buses pick up the Redington children (some of them sons and daughters of my original little cowpunchers) and drive them to departmental schools miles away. When I was no longer needed there I was sent, by my county superintendent, into other remote schools on the cattle ranges of Pima County. Children carry with them a built-in welcome, and I loved other pupils and worked happily with them. But in my heart I took with me the Redington "Little Cowpunchers" as they were called throughout the state and beyond, for the mimeographed school magazine we published every month by that name. They were the models by which I tried — sometimes successfully — to mold later pupils.

My second cow-country school was Baboquivari at Pozo Nuevo, fifty miles south of Tucson. Monday mornings, bitterly cold in winter, I got up at three o'clock to warm the car engine, pack my things, and drive four hours including a stop in the city for errands: servicing the car, leaving the laundry, mailing letters, picking up a week's groceries, and checking on my old friend Lolita who was alone and needed help. I arrived at school at 8:30, disheveled, sleepy, tired; and met twenty-five or more young Mexican livewires of assorted ages and eight grades, all fresh and full of action. Together we rallied under our country's flag and made war, in our fashion, on ignorance, the greatest of all enemies.

In the pattern of Redington, we always had going some extra project to keep our spirits up: a Hallowe'en party, a Christmas program, a rodeo parade, a folksong and dance festival. We even continued publishing "Little Cowpuncher" which won us considerable good publicity. And we went in heavily for art, particularly pottery-making at which my hand-talented pupils excelled. Neither teacher nor children had a moment for idleness.

Came Friday and I highballed it home to tackle the problems that had been cooking there for five days. On the way I had to suffer the wearisome task of shopping and doing ranch errands in Tucson.

At that time Saturday and Sunday was a fleeting period seeming to rate as one day. Then it was that I gave the growing things an extra-good watering, for the men, hoarding water, only sprinkled my plants. After the Cowboy left it was up to me to inspect the animals in the corral and pasture and see as many as I could out on the range. I had to haul hay down to the Windmill Ranch so that the Uncle could ride down and feed any sick animals we had shut up there, and have a bite for his "ole pony." I gave the house a lick and a promise, and did special cooking for the old "pardners" who bunked in the place I had built on to the cabin. Other activities over the weekend were catching up on the mail, having visitors — especially after the advent of the "daughters," mending the roof or the water tank, laundering my clothes, and getting ready for the next 100-mile dash.

Such was my routine in sickness and in health and in all kinds of weather for a long string of years, the last eight of them at Little Mountain School in the Sierritas, forty miles southwest of Tucson. There I found Faye

McGee, mother of three of my schoolboys, who turned out to be just what I needed most — a lifelong friend and a first-class teacher's aide. She saw to it that the school had wood and water and fuel for the oil stove. She drove to town with me when I had to make after-school trips to get school supplies and library books, took me to a movie, bought me refreshments at a drive-in, and drove home that night while I slept. She understood what I was trying to do and pitied me, although I never felt myself an object worthy of pity. I enjoyed being superactive. If I had a second chance at life I would do it over. I have been lucky to have the chance to spend time and energy serving children and cattle. They can be grouped together, for as different as they are, caring for them seems to bring identical problems and satisfactions. Both are prone to all the ills that flesh is heir to. Most of the time none of them knows what is good for him. They all have minds of their own about what they want to do, and with more or less violence, they resent interference and authority. On the other hand, while they are young they are nice to look at and their youthful charms almost always outweigh their obstreperousness. Their possibilities are challenging. Most important of all, there is always something you can do for them.

Of course, if your aim is to get rich you had better not take up either kids or cows, or all the way you will encounter needs greater than your own. But money, say the Spaniards, is like fruit: *no dura* (it doesn't last). You can lay up better treasures. Years of working with children and cattle will bring you self-reliance and resourcefulness, and no day will ever be empty or dull.

When you come up against it, you find the impossible has been overrated. For all the weariness and dowdiness that go with the rush of holding down two jobs and living in two places, there are compensations. Calories or no calories, you never outgrow your clothes. Loneliness is just a word — you have no time to feel its crushing grasp. Activities used for killing time by those, in the words of Dorothy Parker, who like it better dead, have no appeal for you, no meaning. You're busy.

Your satisfaction, after months of steady, mostly cheerful effort, comes on the day of reckoning when you see your calves or your kids stack up well with their contemporaries.

CHAPTER 2

Please Excuse the Pants

January nights are cold even in southern Arizona. Dashing along a Tucson street on the way to a drug store, I was comfortably wrapped, not modishly dressed. The Sunshine Climate Club would have hated me. On top of intimate garments I wore a two-piece red ski undersuit. Over that I had on a pair of Levi's, a man's cashmere shirt, a short woolen coat and a heavy GI pile-lined jacket much too large, belted around me in deep folds. My head was tied up in a red bandana and crowned with a snug-fitting western hat. Woolen socks and stout cowboy boots protected my feet. From a shoulder strap hung an overloaded leather bag.

When I turned the corner at a narrow side street, my swinging purse banged into a well-dressed fellow emerging from a cocktail lounge. Neither of us stopped. I gasped apologetically. He balanced himself, half-turned in stride, and snarled: "Why don't you go back East!"

Me, of all people.

I was still laughing to myself as I drove out of town continuing my hundred-mile night journey. (If a storm threatened, I drove down Sunday night, instead of early Monday morning.) Thinking over the incident to tell friends, all of a sudden it came to me that it wasn't so funny. How did they really feel about the way I dressed? Away from the range, my appearance must often embarrass my associates. Hoodlum calls of "Hi-yo-Silver" and "Yip-pee-E" I could take without notice and feel only the slight annoyance that goes with any encounter with passing rudeness. But well-dressed friends and companions might actually be ashamed to be seen in company of one so unconventionally garbed.

Faye, for instance. I thought: "As we walk down the street, she in her neat print dress, her bare head stylishly coiffed, and I in Levi's, boots, and Stetson, how does she feel when she meets friends and has to say: 'This is our teacher'?"

I spent the remainder of my journey driving back to school mentally drawing up a brief.

It was consolation to recollect that independent characters who dress for their personal comfort and convenience, rather than for the approval of the public, have been shocking the populace since the human race lost hirsute hides and simian appendages. I thought of the scandal caused by the "bloomer" girls. Farther back, the man who first divided his nether garment into twin cylinders to fit his bifurcated anatomy must have been lonely among the robed and toga-ed. But who likes to be lonely? One must have a good reason to risk being shunned. I appreciated with regret the fortitude and charity it took to be friends with a nonconformist like me, a woman in Levi's.

Actually the man I bumped had a right to be indignant at my bulk and awkwardness; but his judgment was hasty. It was downright poor. Whatever I am, the West produced me. And I was not trying to make a spectacle of myself. I had nothing but business on my mind. With trade as my purpose I was not dressed to pass inspection by style-conscious bystanders. I was dressed for a long night ride in an unheated pickup. Nevertheless, there I was under the bright lights, sticking out like a finger-splint, jostling evening strollers and shocking one into ill-founded criticism.

Whether you dress to be comfortable or to be attractive depends on how busy you are, where you work, and the chronological point of life to which you have attained. In early youth, I confess, I tried to look like other girls. To be in style I bared my calves and clavicles during the years I studied and taught in the city. For a glamorous decade I tried to keep up with the vogue: skimpy skirts, cobwebby hose, uncovered head. And I paid for this effort to put on style by constant illness during spells of bad weather. Then I moved into the country, and learned to be comfortable — and the heck with fashion.

It was a blessing to find relief from the respiratory ailments — ear ache, sore throat, congested nose and sinuses, tonsilitis and bronchitis that had plagued me since childhood. I learned that adequate clothing protected my health, for I discovered — with the help of an astute young doctor, that I was subject to an allergy to cold — the temperature cold, opposite of heat. Whoever heard of such a thing? True it is, though, and it condemns me socially to a grasshopper existence — bright and gay only in fair weather. In the heat of Arizona summers I can gussie up in skirts and other feminine frills. If the occasion demands, I can cut off my jeans below the pockets and tan my legs as other women do. But even in summer I must avoid drafts, damp clothes, and high-voltage cooling systems. Comes frost. *Br-r-r!* My pants and boots. Real winter sets in. *Br-r-r,* fortissimo! My long-handles and pile-lined jacket. For worse than hurt vanity, embarrassed friends, and an outraged Mrs. Grundy is an aching head and the creeping upward curse of cold, cold feet.

When I voided my teaching contract with the city by getting married, it was my good luck that the county school superintendent had a better opinion of conjugal status than her city counterpart. The latter, and the school board he influenced, never seemed to realize when marriage was banned for women teachers (men teachers of course were allowed to wed), that babies are what keep up tax-supported schools. This is not said in bitterness, for he did me a favor by his decree. Eventually it sent me to Redington, an environment made to order for persons such as I. There, while mentoring my "little cowpunchers," I found physical comfort by shielding my body against the climate. The great open country was alive with horses and cowboys, and pupils with extra mounts who wanted teacher to help "round up the pasture." Having to be ready at dismissal bell, I dared to teach the three R's while dressed in boots, Levi's and shirts with plenty of pockets. A side effect was the exorcising of my demons of affliction. No runny nose. No loss of voice. And with reasonable caution no migraine headaches. I had found my niche. I have never left it, patterning my life to the all-weather uniform of boots, sombrero, and what goes between.

It was never my purpose to start a fashion or even a fad when I made local history by wearing pants into the schoolroom. But for succeeding years, and in each different school, as soon as I put aside pretty dresses and came to school in Levi's, the girls in my classes followed suit. I don't remember that anything was ever said about it, but when frosty mornings arrived every leg in the room was covered with heavy dark-blue jeans. Apparently the mothers accepted the idea as good. And it certainly saved laundering, always a problem in a community such as Sierrita where there was a constant water shortage. It not only helped keep the girls warm but it gave them more freedom in such activity as playing baseball.

Every departure from the ordinary must be accompanied by complications and sacrifices. Some of my school patrons

frowned on having a teacher who dressed "like a man" until they got used to me. I dreaded shocking the school superintendent whose once-a-year visits were never scheduled so that none knew at what moment she might pop in. The late winter day she came I'm sure she was startled by my appearance (for which I made no apology or explanation), but my marvelous little cowpunchers put on such a good performance for her that she approved us all and said nothing about my overclad feet and legs. Later she met an itinerant maker of movie shorts and sent him out to make a newsreel of our little school and its projects. And she herself came again, this time for an overnight visit, and brought with her a woman feature writer for the Tucson morning paper. As we three sat before the open fire in my snug little teacherage, I entertained them — off the record, I thought — with accounts of road troubles I'd had on account of river floods, gully washouts, car breakdowns at night, and being stuck to the axles in mud.

To my chagrin, the Sunday paper, which eventually found its way (by the trice-weekly mail car coming down from Benson) over the mountains, contained a half-page yarn about the great pioneering work I was doing in the wilderness of the San Pedro River Valley. I was ashamed to show my face to the mothers, the true pioneers in the district. My closest neighbor and dear friend (mother of five — the youngest she'd had by herself during an isolating flood while her husband was away on the roundup) remarked, as I sneaked into her kitchen where she was ironing with sad irons by a kerosene lamp and getting supper for eight over a wood fire while minding the babies:

"Don't we live in a terrible place and ain't you wonderful!"

The biggest problem of a trousered female teacher is a trip to the city. At teachers' meetings I conformed and suffered the consequences — such as a flat tire on the road; to change it I had to take off my skirt and hose. On Friday afternoon visits to the county library in the superintendent's office, there simply wasn't time to change into a dress. Looking straight ahead in a purposeful manner, I strode in, lugging a heavy box of books, and busied myself at the shelves selecting replenishments, speaking only to those with the courage to greet me first.

One afternoon years ago the assistant superintendent confronted me thusly: "Do you know you are breaking the law?"

Laughingly she showed me a volume of city ordinances, among them an old blue law making it illegal for a woman to appear on the streets of Tucson dressed in men's clothing. Laughing myself, I showed her that I happened on this occasion to be wearing women's denim riders one of the "daughters" had given me. Ordinarily I never use them because they have no hip pockets into which I can slip the metal case containing my reading glasses.

After a while, as with most eccentrics, people got used

to me and I was kindly tolerated. Once there was a combined meeting of city and county teachers that I didn't know about ahead of time. Fortunately coats were long in those days. I buttoned mine, rolled my pants up above my knees, and sincerely hoped when I was greeted by my former principal that he didn't know I was not "dressed."

When the Cowboy became the head of my household there were other complications. He objected to my pants if worn anywhere off the ranch. That was long before capri pants and stretch pants and he certainly had precedent on his side. In usual circumstances, even yet, the ranks of women connected with the cattle business who wear pants in public are very thin indeed. Mary Kidder Rak, in her book *Cowman's Wife,* explains that ranch women are delighted at any chance to break the monotony by dressing up and looking feminine. True enough. They do not have my affliction. Besides, they are representing their husbands. A cowman, whatever he may think about others' frontier pants and cowgal rigging, wants his wife to have on the prettiest dress in town, and most of them can afford the best.

Man's authority to dictate — even legislate — what women wear extends back to Adam who doubtless designed Eve's girdle of figleaves. There are good reasons for this. What woman does not like to give her man pleasure at the sight of her?

Before marriage, the man of the outfit said: "You look nice in any old rag." After marriage he said: "Why don't you look like other women?"

There were three great big reasons. Money was the first. We were trying to exist as well as build up the place — watering holes, fences, saddlehorses, bulls, materials and supplies — on approximately $2400 a year. My health was the second. Even a short trip in the unheated rattletrap car sans pants and boots, and I was sick. My habit of feeling at-the-ready only in work clothes was the third. This habit developed because emergencies are the rule once you get out of sight of civilization. The car lights went out one night and I walked two miles up the canyon bed with nothing between me and the scratching, crawling sand and a possibly-lurking rattlesnake, but high-heeled white sandals. One moonlight night I lost half of my load of hay on a quick turn and ruined my best hose heaving it back on the little truck. The blue dress capped the climax.

I had been on a business trip to the land department and was arrayed in my sheer blue dress that made my eyes look blue. It was sprigged with figures in two shades of darker blue and had bows and a belt of the darkest blue. My big hat of fine soft straw was trimmed with velvet ribbons of the same three lovely shades. I even wore gloves — dark blue to match my pumps. Returning late that afternoon, I ran into a crisis at Mesquite Corral, two miles down the canyon from headquarters. The Cowboy had been working cattle alone all day, an exasperating job if ever there was one, and was now locked in battle with a big steer he had tied down and was attempting to dehorn by trimming off a corner of each side of the victim's skull with a little saw he carried tied to his saddle. Fool-like, I stopped the car, shed my gloves, and went over to see if I could maybe hold a rope or hand him something. His sweaty face was red with passion. His shirt was red with blood.

"Get on his neck!" he cried without a glance at me.

"But my dress," I faltered.

"Get on his neck, damn it!" he shouted.

I got on his neck, damn it. A fountain of blood splattered the sheer blue dress that made my eyes look blue. In the scuffle my pretty hat with the blue ribbons was

knocked off my head and landed in a splash of soft green manure.

The slow bitter turning of the years brought changes. To him — the right to identify himself with a woman who looks smart in that special meaning of the word: "stylish, spruce, showy, up-to-date." To me — the independence to dress as my purse, my person, and my work direct and no sham pretenses involved.

Once a year I am right in style. That is during February in Tucson's pre-rodeo days when all on the streets are required to wear cowboy rigging or suffer durance vile at the hands of the vigilante committee (Junior Chamber of Commerce).

One Saturday morning I happened to pass two teenagers loitering in front of a movie theater apparently killing time while waiting for it to open its doors, by remarking about the girls and women dressed in rodeo style who happened to pass by. Evidently I didn't rate much. As I came abreast I heard the older boy say thoughtfully, "No, but I'll bet she has a horse!"

CHAPTER 3

Water Comes First

When fate in the form of a younger, fairer girl de-spoused me, I sought a substitute teacher for my little cowpunchers and became, for a time (until I could get things going and find someone who would stay on the place while I was off at work) solely a woman-with-a-little-ranch: actually, a woman-about-to-lose-a-little-ranch. The odds were overwhelming. No help, no capital, no credit, and — the greatest of all handicaps — no rain. But when everything is against you, when you haven't got a ghost of a show, the injustice of the battle enrages you to superhuman endurance and fighting strength.

When I read *Gone With The Wind* I was greatly touched by the pluck of Scarlett O'Hara, determined to save her beloved Tara, the plantation where she was born, with her bare hands. In my case, "Tara" was a little raw-hide outfit that added up economically to nothing but hard work and hard luck. Sentimentally it totaled more. It was the home of my cows and horses and dogs; my own roots had dug in there for seven dry years. I couldn't abandon it.

Strictly speaking, I had not been in the management branch of the operation. I was part of the crew of which the Cowboy had been the better half. I had *helped* brand and doctor cattle and gather and deliver them; and *helped* build fences and corrals and sheds; and haul feed and supplies; and fix roads; and put in and maintain wells and troughs and pipelines. But I had looked to authority for direction. My main job had been a hundred miles farther south.

Then one day, there I was alone — the whole shebang on my shoulders. Where to begin? Like a student, I tried to survey the situation by writing down a schedule of the duties I must undertake, in what I considered their order of importance.

First came water. Check the tanks. Start the pump. Go down the canyon five miles to the deep well, and repeat.

Second, the critters — the livestock, beginning with the hospitalized ones.

Third in rank, the people, if any. Friends and relatives and occasional hired hands must at times be housed and fed and transported, and even kept amused.

Fourth, I listed outdoor chores: fences, *represos* (dams), corrals, roadwork, wood-getting, business and shopping trips to the outside.

Fifth, tasks that were purely pleasure: trees, vines, flowers, garden, and care of pets.

Beyond that, unexpended energy for housework and personal activities such as reading and writing.

Sheer necessity put water first. Water — the loveliest and most powerful of earth's compounds, most remarkable of Nature's agents — wonder-working water, to keep alive my nearly two hundred head of livestock and the growing plants in my quarter-acre garden. Water, from that day forward, became my responsibility.

This arresting thought, with all its ramifications, sent me to a small encyclopedia that opened its discourse with this sentence: "The importance of water to life and most of its properties is familiar to all."

I met this statement with skepticism. I wondered how

many of "all" those living in municipalities in our land ever think beyond the convenience of water taps and the annoyance of bills, or how familiar they are with the plight of the rural minority who invite disaster by owning their own water systems.

An urbanite woman, by a twist of the wrist, is painlessly supplied with the precious stuff which refreshes her, inside and out. She is uneasy only when it comes down upon her in shelterless moments in some form of precipitation. She doesn't know how well-off she is to be able to obtain bodily comfort and peace of mind merely by opening a faucet. She never has had to manipulate a mechanical motor-driven pump or pull the sucker rods of a windmill. She has never worked a "one-armed Johnny" or pulled water out of a dug well with a bucket on the end of a rope and watched the dry cows swig it down faster than she could bring it up.

Now and then, in society and in business, I meet her and she says she envies my outdoor life in the great open spaces. My boots and pants and heavily tanned skin intrigue her. In her innocence she cannot imagine the pitfalls lying in wait if she were to forsake the city waterworks for the "freedom" of life on a cattle ranch. The freedom is relative. She would find herself a slave to the tedious, sometimes perilous task of keeping water where it is needed.

Each night in the six months of Southern Arizona "summer" I have to go down the canyon three-quarters of a mile in a rough pickup to fight the pump into action. No matter what the fix I am in physically or emotionally, what I have done during the day, how far I have traveled or how late arrived home (once it was 2:30 a.m.), I must go down the bumpy lonesome road and wrestle the pump. I cannot wait until daylight, because the pipeline is on top of the ground — the ground being ninety-nine percent rocks. Three to six hours of pumping under the Arizona sun would result in a tank of scalding water. Also, it is easier on the engine to run it at night. It is not easier on the engineer.

On occasion during school terms, I have stayed awake all night to drive a hundred miles after work to start the pump, fill the tanks, and water the trees. Then retrace the hundred miles to be on hand to ring the opening school bell in the morning.

It is a matter of water or no water. If you have cows and horses and plants, there is no compromise. Death may strike, banks go broke, hearts break, earthquakes heave, bombs explode — the pump must keep on putting out water.

A pump is something to regard with ambivalence. I love to hear one run (the motor, of course). It is musical rhythm with soothing lyrics that seem to say: *WATER, water, water, water* — *WATER, water, water, water,* hour after morale-building hour. To an outdoor Arizonan, it can be nothing but pleasant. But a pump is more than that. Literally, says my dictionary, a pump is "a mechanical device for raising, circulating, or otherwise moving, or for compressing or exhausting, a liquid or gas, by means of suction or pressure, usually induced by the motion of a lever or crank." The word I get out of that is *exhausting.* No contraption ever devised by man produces more corollary exhaustion than a stationary gasoline engine.

When Roger Bannister broke the four-minute mile, magazines printed pictures of him collapsing into the arms of his pals at the end of his run. He looked the way I feel after a bout with a balky engine. But such a contest could never be considered sport. It is too unequal: an eight and one-half-horsepower motor versus the human heart, horsepower about 1/240.

It is consoling to know that women have no monopoly on trouble with engines. The mine up my canyon has a number of stationary engines. Every few days the three mechanics on hire are going to the mat with one or more of them, and sometimes, even like me, coming out second best. It has struck my notice that few mechanics are men past middle life. Their mortality rate must be high, suggesting that engine trouble is a deadly hazard — the reason, no doubt, for the excessive hourly wage mechanics have to be paid.

The pump itself rarely goes out of kilter. When it does need a part, if only a cheap gasket, you can't go to the place where you bought it. You must send far away, to Salem, Ohio. If you don't have the foresight and cash to order essentials like rings and valve stems before you need them, your water supply is imperiled. The transaction takes weeks.

Nothing more curse-worthy than the gasoline engine has been invented in the name of progress. After it has run fifty hours, there is only one way for it to go — down the hill to the repair shop. In my case, this means over a hundred miles of travel and most of an uneasy day watching mechanics monkey around at four dollars an hour. The hardest part of the operation is the loading and unloading of the dead-iron weight. For ruin of health and temper and morale, and devastation of expense funds, I will back a little one-cylinder gasoline engine against any game of chance. I know a successful cowman — one who lends the bank money instead of vice versa — who goes to superstitious lengths never to approach one. He says, with appropriate invective, "I can just ride by one and it stops."

A sister from a California city, visiting at the Ranch in November, went with me one morning when I drove down to start the pump. The spring is a lovely place, the beauty spot of the ranch: clear, running water edged by dwarf sycamores under high conglomerate bluffs decorated with sahuaros, ocotillos, and *nopales*. Under a shabby tin roof by this murmuring stream, sits the scowling untidy iron monster that lifts the water, when it will, a distance of 4300 feet and a height of almost 300 feet into the big cement tank which supplies the house, garden, and corral pipelines.

While she stood impressed, I filled the gas tank, checked the oil, primed the pump, flipped the choke lever, took up the crank, and gave the heavy flywheel about twenty jerking whirls — one by one. Nothing happened.

I removed the sparkplug, scraped it with my knife, poured some gas into the head, and then cranked it another twenty times. It was flooded. I kept cranking until it lost compression. Again I took out the sparkplug and this time poured in a few drops of oil. When I picked up the handle again, I ignored my sister, spoke a few coarse words, and went at it with my whole strength like a dog at furious attack. It exploded into action, noisy and smoking, lifting my spirits and ready to lift water. I cheerfully threw in the clutch, adjusted the gas, felt the intake pipe to make sure it was pumping, then washed my hands of it.

The next day when I started down to the pump, my sister said firmly: "I'll stay here and clean the kitchen. I can't stand to see you start the pump."

One morning, particularly beat by the 135 strenuous muscular wrenches it had taken to get the engine going, I sat staring at it in puzzled contemplation. Why are internal-combustion engines, whose motive power is caused by the explosion of a mixture of air and gas, so hard to keep in order? Why hasn't some smart inventor put his know-how to work on them? Why don't industrialists

develop a product that will give reasonable service without a high-priced mechanic fooling with them every few days? Thus pondering, I asked aloud in my privacy of several square miles: "I wonder who first made the half-baked s.o.b.?"

The encyclopedia divulged some facts. The first gas-burning engine was made in 1823 by Samuel Brown, who used it to propel a boat on the Thames, drive a carriage, and work a pump. (Not that he needed a pump: he was just playing.) It didn't amount to anything — merely Mr. Brown's hobby-horse. The first commercially practicable one, operating on illuminating gas, was placed on the market by the Frenchman, Lenoir, in 1860. It was discarded because it used so much gas. In 1877, Nikolaus Otto patented the prototype of the four-cycle internal-combustion gasoline engine we use today.

But gasoline engines to pump water belong to the age of bustles and high-wheeled bicycles! Oh! that in the near future I might turn in my own mulish unreliable apparatus on a snappy, wonder-metal, lightweight gasoline engine that would fire at the press of a button and run for years the way my little pickup has — nearly five years and 94,000 miles with no motor repairs, not even a valve job.

But, Dr. Otto, I guess I'm stuck with you. And so are all my fellow-ranchers from the hills and backwoods, at least until the whole country is powered by something that doesn't require miles of wire and poles.

Excluding hill and canyon country such as this, as far as I know, the United States already relies on electric motors for power. I pass them in the agricultural valleys, and stop in wonder to see solid streams of water as wide as I am shooting out of big pipes that go deep into the earth. It seems a miracle. As I drive along the city streets

I notice the misty spray from lawn sprinklers and am struck by its delicate beauty; also I am comforted with the knowledge that the woman's hand that turned it on need not be grimed with oil and carbon that go too deep for soap.

Electric power has crept like a rising flood into the rural sections of our land. Once it looked as if it might creep into my place. A co-op representative came around taking applications, and I put in mine with the filing fee of five dollars. The company started up, and went as far as a millionaire's ranch just this side of the great mountains. Then came a Republican Congress, and my participation in REA blew up. (I never got back my five dollars, either.)

But even electricity cannot prevent pipeline troubles. Rust, for example, eats iron enough to shorten the lifespan of a mile of two-inch pipe which would cost about four thousand dollars to replace. As time goes by, there are increasing holes to plug in my waterline. Since it must be above ground — this ground is too solid to be ditched — the twenty-foot lengths are welded so that when heat expands them they can squirm around without breaking at the joints.

One year, in the midst of our mild winter rainy season, the atmosphere split open, north and south, as with the rod of Moses. Down the opening came a two-day blast of arctic cold that froze all the pipelines in the country, and broke most of them; mine, I believe, took the record. Surprise, rather than carelessness, caused our disaster. That January tenth was sunny and mild as usual; we rode without jackets. But that evening, a warning by radio made me send the Nephew down to drain the line by opening the faucet at the pump. There is a theory in this part of the world that as long as water is moving it won't freeze. The faucet was opened part way so that it would drain slowly all night, and it wouldn't take so long to fill the line next morning.

Before daylight Old North Pole puffed up his cheeks with icy air and blew a blast straight at the desert country of the Southwest. Neighbors will testify that never before had a barrel cactus been known to freeze. To the dismayed astonishment of all, even the giant sahuaros — many of them ancient — were killed. Nobody had seen that happen before.

Our old pipeline? At first count there were ninety-three breaks ranging from pencil-sized holes to splits four feet long. It was eight days before we got water to the house and then only a trickle. We used a truckload of old inner tubes which we cut into strips and wrapped tightly over the breaks, binding the rubber at close intervals with plier-tightened lengths of baling wire. Later, when the weather cleared and we had some water storage to rely on, we cemented the worst breaks, carrying heavy buckets of sand and cement up and down the gullies.

I say "we," for this disaster did not have to be tackled single-handed. The Nephew, with a few weeks of free time, was visiting. And we were re-enforced by a kind neighbor: Pete, the caretaker at an idle copper mill up the canyon, who devised some clamps patterned after the high priced ones I had bought in town for the most strategic spots. His pipes were broken, too, but his line was short enough to fix in a couple of days and he had pipe replacements.

While we were laboring to get water up on the hill, we had to catch rainwater off the roof for house use, and had to take time out from the pipe work to drive the cattle down the creek to the spring.

Electricity would have helped in this calamity. A friend

who lives in the village offered to bring his paraphernalia and weld the breaks; thus getting water up here faster and with much less hard work. But no electric power. Long ago, when the mine up the creek was a million-dollar operation, they had a big generator — its drive shaft weighed four and a half tons, according to the junk man who blew it up with dynamite and trucked it to Los Angeles — and thus plenty of electricity. Long ago, that was. All the machinery has since been trucked away for scrap iron. The wire is gone, and the only poles remaining are those in inaccessible places.

Some day, when the world is in need of the minerals in this extremely rough location, that is, when the minerals are vital enough to warrant the terrific expense necessary to transport them, there will be electric power in this canyon again. But not in my day. For me there is no escape from Dr. Otto's bungling. But there are compensations.

I know of no better way to assuage the melancholia known in recent times as "carrying the torch," than to tackle a gasoline engine in an ugly condition. You may be sad in the gray dawn as you listlessly don your work togs. They are greasy and torn. Who's to care? You stumble down the steep path to the great cottonwood you have loved for years and whose loveliness and color was once a shared pleasure. There is no roughhousing in the canyon sand, no tricks or jokes to lift morale above the dreaded task.

As your nostalgic glance moves up the empty trail while you are straining the gas into the tank and checking the oil level, a ghost on horseback meets memory's eye. Instinctively you listen for a whistle that you know you'll never hear again: *Avaunt, shade! Dr. Otto, quick, our duel!*

You place the crank, spraddle your legs, stoop low to the level of your monstrous enemy, place the fingers of your left hand over the apertures forming the choke, push the intake valve with your thumb, and with the right hand and arm spin the heavy, solid wheel full blast, releasing the valve and choke at what you hope is the propitious moment. Nothing happens. Repeat operation. Same result. Do this again and again; strain and work and worry and fight. When at last the recalcitrant contraption has yielded into heart-warming explosions, you are so played out you have a good immunity to emotional hangovers. That ghost, you reflect philosophically, as your heart stops palpitating, you wipe the sweat from your brow, and trudge uphill to open the valves, was a darn poor pumpman also.

CHAPTER 4

My Trouble with Men

The usual man-trouble that every woman is heir to has no place in this chronicle. My bill of particulars is here alleged against the sturdy male — age under-fifteen to over-fifty — who, out of pity, or for the mere pittance I can dig up to pay, or in response to the call of the vast outdoor romance of range country, has fallen by chance into the small world of my authority, *mi ranchito.*

Before making my complaint, let me express under solemn vow my sincere gratitude, and make a haphazardly hasty attempt to give the devil his due. That it is a man's world will be denied by no one but men, and even then *in sincerity* by only a handful of henpecked husbands. If it isn't a man's world, *Homo sapiens* does not have his just rights, for he is the most interesting, masterful, and in many ways the most admirable phenomenon of creation.

From the cradle he feels superior to all women. With reason. He has advantages that females can only envy. By nature, he is endowed with a power that makes clear to him, such incomprehensibles as mercury switches, up-draft carburetors, venturis, and torsion-bar suspension. Formulae, slide-rules, railroad timetables, ropes, shovels, axes, instructions that come with stationary engines — all make sense and become sufficient in his naturally competent hands. Instinctively, he can drive a nail without choking up on the hammer.

Note also that he is by birthright a stout fellow. From the time he kicks the slats out of his crib and pounds his mother with his fists, he strongly out-muscles womankind. I have watched in bitter envy a man no taller than I and only fifty or sixty pounds heavier deftly toss a bale of hay up to the fifth tier. I have been astounded to see a schoolboy not much more than half my size and with a fiftieth part of my experience neatly wrench a tire off its rim.

Besides these and similar gifts of intellect, brawn, and skill, men excel socially — if only to make horses and kids behave. If the legendary world of the Amazons was not altogether mythical, it is plain why it did not endure. You have heard, I am sure, of women horse-breakers. You may have seen pictures of them, or have seen them in person displaying their mounts. I, for one, have never seen a mount so trained that was not a high-stepping, head-slinging rascal prone to playfulness that did not stop at dislodging his rider once in a while for the fun of it. And as to bringing up children, I can testify that one of the banes of the schoolroom is a mama's boy.

Speaking from the West, where men — by legend and main force — retain their original *status supremus,* I am ready to concede that it is good that they do inherit the earth they populate. I know how wonderful and how necessary they are. I know the other side of them, too.

As for getting one to work for you if you are a woman, you are asking for conflict you may have least expected. The female boss is a circumstance man has encountered too recently in history to have adjusted to taking it in stride. It is against his tradition; contrary to his inclination; fatal to his aspiration as a member of the ruling sex and it takes money applied with tact to make him suffer it. Perhaps enough money might make him like it; nothing else will. Shoving into a composite specimen the run of transient and would-be cowboys who have allowed me to hire them, (this excepts the "oldies" who have been the real nucleus of the establishment and have gratefully accepted a woman's place as being better than no place at all) I note regretfully that his response to a command or entreaty is forever evasive and oblique. Before he can comply he has to take measures to counterbalance his masculine complexes.

"Bill," I call, "come here and hold this wrench."

Curious, Bill comes readily. Will he pick up the wrench and hold it in the way and place I indicate? Ha, ha! He has to negotiate and assert. What am I doing and why do I want to do it?

From plenty of practice, I stifle warlike impulses and lay down my wrench and the bolt and the nut. I explain and argue. He can think of a better idea, but if I am patient and genial and keep him happy, I may get my way. Bill is sixteen. Tom, Dick, and Harry have been most of the other ages.

I have nostalgic memories of girl helpers — college girls wanting to stand in for men who had gone to the wars — who followed my lead and let me make my mistakes in peace. Of dozens of men, I can think of only two who have felt obliged to take orders and paychecks from the same source: Wilbur took pains to do things exactly as I directed, and the good Uncle often said, with obvious reservations of male opinion: "Well, if that's the way you want it, that's the way I'll do it."

But the Uncle was never a hired hand. It happened that out of mutual need and his chivalrous sympathy for underdogs and women in distress, he adopted me, and with the attitude of a partner, did his best for the place he picked out to be his home during the last eighteen years of his long life.

He drew no wages. Experienced by a half-century of working with cow outfits, he would hopefully ask when we shipped our calves: "Did we get enough to pay up?"

In a way, I inherited this good old man who was known to the countryside as "Uncle Jim," and he turned out to be a legacy more precious than gold. When the Cowboy moved from his homestead down the canyon up to head-quarters as the Man-on-the-Place, he hired the Uncle — whom I did not know until then — for twenty dollars a month and "keep," to stay on the abandoned Windmill Ranch in his stead. "Keep" amounted to so little I was ashamed to be a party to it. Weekends I cooked a roast or a stew and a big pie and took them down to him with a few canned goods to pep up his regular diet of biscuits, beans, jerky, and syrup. I didn't suspect how much he appreciated it. When the Cowboy flew the coop and the Uncle went back to his old job as watchman for a little business (service station, commissary, and bar) in the village, he told Vi (the friendly young woman who worked there) when they were discussing me: "Talk about your good cooks, now there's a good cook!" I had guessed right; he *was* hungry. And never did bread I cast upon the waters bring better return.

Left alone, I struggled beyond my capacity for three months. In November I was trying to brand the big spring calves. It was more than I could handle alone, and I didn't have money to hire help. One day I met Uncle Jim in the postoffice.

"How you gittin' along?" he asked so solicitously that I could not hold back the tears.

"Don't worry," he said. "I'm trying' to git me a little pension, and when I git it I'll go down and he'p you."

He was considered too old to work, long before I met him. Ten years later I saw him put in day after day of hard labor afoot and on horseback, and he wanted to do it. Soon after he was installed as my "pardner," The Old Cowman, chief adviser who was never around when real labor was taking place, counseled: "Git rid of that old feller. He'll git too old on you and git down and you'll have to take care of him."

"I only hope I get the chance!" I answered.

I did. He stayed with me until the last. The final three years he lived, he did not realize how dependent he had become, or that the man I hired for $100 a month (when I was working for $150 and love of my job) was there to take care of him. When he did understand that he could no longer do for himself, he died in spite of all I could do.

The fall he came to "he'p," he took over the chore routine when we got the calves branded and watched the outfit so that I could go back to school. He was the luckiest thing that ever happened to me as a ranch-keeper. His services were beyond the humiliation-tainted barter of human sweat for cash. His pension was small, but since the ranch furnished his livelihood and that of his beloved bay horse, his needs amounted to little more than pipe tobacco, a quart of whiskey a week, a Sunday hat every three or four years, and now and then some denim pants and jackets. Birthdays and Christmas took care of his shirts and small items. He never considered coins as being money. When we went to town and he came home with a pocket full of change, he'd put it away in tobacco cans to give to the schoolboys who came to stay with us in summertime. He was never broke — my usual condition. When I started out on a business trip, he would pull out his wallet and say: "Do you need any money?" The ranch dogies were his. They grew up to be mother cows, so he always had a few calves to sell.

The Uncle's greatest value to the little ranch was that

he loved it. Its troubles were his troubles. He gave it the loyalty we save for the last things of earth we cling to. And always he was my friend. He never intruded in my personal life, or tried to take part in the things that interested me outside the ranch. We did not read the same books, or — except for newscasts — enjoy the same radio programs. Our relationship was that of two self-respecting people who respected each other and kept a decent reserve between them. It comforted me to know that whatever happened, however wrong I was, he was on my side. Nobody said anything against me in his presence. If I got into trouble, he, in his words, "takened it up."

Naturally he had the limitations arising from a long hard life. He was no good at any kind of night job because he couldn't see after dark. And he was seriously afflicted with "rheumatics." He did the best he could, and was always there tending to the place; nothing more was expected of him.

But at certain times of the year and in emergencies, it was necessary to hire a man or two. There began my trouble with men.

If you are a woman with an income of two or three thousand dollars a day from oil wells and are ranching just for romance, you can sit in luxury in your western low-roofed castle, call the bunkhouse by intercom system to give directions to the foreman, and spend a great deal of money hiring and firing men who jeer at you behind your back. (Such a woman was for a time my neighbor.)

On the other hand, if you are existing on a shoestring with little hope of gaining prosperity, and haven't sense enough to give up and quit, you'll have to solve manpower crises with something besides cash.

When the necessity arises, and you go looking for help from the stronger sex, you give yourself a talking-to. You will be tactful. You will keep to the sidelines and let him take over as much as possible. You will assert your check-book-right with the utmost diplomacy and *never* say *frog* when you want him to jump.

If the available cowboy (or reasonable facsimile) is young, he will want to rip and snort. He will try to ride and rope in a dashing manner with little regard for the cattle on the other end of his jaunty action. Odds are, he will already have what knowledge he thinks he needs about the cow business; he has learned it from TV or at the big outfit he worked for (and was fired from), and they "done it this-a-way." He wants a free hand with plenty of horses and plenty of cattle, and a car to use after work.

"Look, cowboy," you say, "play it cool. We don't want to cripple the old horses or booger the cattle. I have to keep these old cows gentle so that I can work them alone. Take it easy. Don't crowd them. Talk to them, whistle at them. Don't run at them swinging your rope. Let's ease them up to the corrals and catch them on foot."

That loses you your man (right now or as soon as he has traveling money). You are the one who is going to get the job done, and it will gall him to poke along being flunky to a cranky old woman.

You let him rope the calves when you get to the corrals, and tie them down, and you keep your mouth shut when several of them get up. But when you insist on doing the branding yourself — because you use a really hot iron, smacking it down fast in the interest of mercy — and assign him the disagreeable task of keeping up the fire, your employee-management relations have "blowed up."

And do not imagine that the remedy is simply to find a not-young cowpuncher. The older ones, if any are avail-able, *know* all right. They were born to work, and don't know there is any other way to live. But as long as they are able-bodied, in these times they have good steady jobs to pick and choose from. Those available to small-timers like me are broken-down old fellows who still want to do what they no longer can. You have to look out for them while they're doing the stock work. It is easy to get one hurt or killed.

Old Perry, when he voluntarily came to help me out while the Uncle was hospitalized from a malignant tumor, did not know that he was "riding the chuck line." He thought he was putting in time until his "very-coarse veins" cleared up so his legs would be well enough to permit him to get on the roster of some good outfit again. He had run several big ones in his day. Sadly I considered the fifty years and more he had devoted himself to making cattle pay for the big livestock companies. Now that he was deaf and crippled, he had been turned out to die like an old horse. I pitied him for being reduced to my size. But on his part, there was no question of gratitude. He thought he was doing me a real favor. In his heart he had only contempt for little outfits. His talk was big. He had dealt in steers by the thousands. So it didn't matter, I soon learned, if a few of them died every day or two.

He made fun of me for my lavish use of smears and sprays. Why, when he worked for the So-and-So's (in high-mountain country, I knew), they never doctored a case of worms in the fifteen years he was there. In nine days the "bugs" just fell out!

He was honest and brave and tried to help. It was my hard luck that he couldn't make a hand because he was infirm and would make no compromises with his infirmities.

One cold windy day we saddled up to drive a bunch of cows off several miles to where there was still some grass. He didn't know the country and took little notice of my efforts to brief him on the job. He knew how to drive cattle! Why, he was driving cattle before I was born!

I took the lead down a long winding canyon, and Perry kept them coming, hollering and singing and popping the end of his rope against his chaps to move the drags. I stopped at the point where we were to turn them up the ridge. That was his signal to come around the side to me and help push them out on the mesa. When he kept driving them into me, I yelled and waved and fought the astonished cows. He never looked up, but kept driving. I had to let the cattle go; climb around to him and plant myself in his face; and yell at the top of my voice that *THAT WAS THE PLACE.*

He couldn't hear it thunder, but he would not watch to see if I motioned to him. On rounds to gather the calves for branding, I tried to figure out some prearranged signals with my arms and hat. He was cold to such as that. He told me a story about a boss he had one time, who, when they went out together, would ride up on a high place and yell at Perry, then point down into a steep brushy draw. Perry would ride through the thorny bushes and over the steep rocky gullies and bring out the little bunch of cattle. The boss, still up there like a statue, would point over a steep ridge into another rough gulch, dark with spiny thickets. Perry would go in and dig out the cattle. One day Perry rode up on the high point where the boss was stationed, pulled him off his horse, and punched him in the nose.

A cousin offered to stay with old Perry when the Christmas holidays were over and I had to go back to school. The old fellow had plenty of fault to find with the way I ran cattle, and relieved his mind to the cousin, who had plenty of time to listen. Perry said that if I'd turn the ranch over to him, he'd make some money out of that little bunch of nellies. Only on condition — he wanted it understood — that I stay down at that school and leave him alone. The poor old fellow was already moribund. Two years later I helped bury him.

Formal education helps smooth the male's problem of being "told" by a woman. Two young college graduates holding executive positions at a mine up the creek were visting the ranch when someone dropped the top of a lotion bottle into the lavatory sink so that it exactly fit, and was too far down to be grasped by any tool. The young men were trying various methods of gouging when I came along. "I wonder if the plumber's friend would get it?" I suggested.

The suction worked. The boys exchanged amused secret-order glances and smiles and muttered something I didn't quite catch about ". . . trust a woman . . ."

If you do anything at all, you are bound to err — especially on rangeland. When you do succeed in an endeavor, you are fool enough to wish for credit but not fool enough to expect it from range men. Even if it's good, they resent it.

Late one day a man came in his truck, wanting to buy a two-year-old mule from me. I had got a broken arm teaching her to lead, and was not anxious to continue tutoring her. But I didn't think we could load her before dark, although she was already in the main corral. The cocky young cowboy who was with the buyer spoke up, declaring he would bet me $5.00 he could load her alone before dark. I said "all right," and the buyer and I climbed up on the corral fence to watch.

The cowboy put his rope on little Jessie and led her around and around. She was on to that. I watched with pride. But when he opened the little gate in the corner and tried to lead her into the small crowding chute, she quit him. He tried over and over. Nothing doing. It began to get dark. He began to get mad. He snubbed the long rope over a post in the chute wall, got behind her, and whipped her with the rope's doubled end. She humped up and took the whipping. He didn't kick her then, for she was in position to kick back. Finally he tightened the rope and choked her down. She lay broadside in the dusk, gasping loudly against strangulation, while he kicked her now — in the back, the belly, and the head. I jumped down and ran with a big bucket of water from the trough and dashed it on her head. She jumped up, and lunged into the chute and on up into the truck in one wild movement. The cowboy's only comment: "That's a goddam mule for you."

There must be some deeply buried reason why it annoys a man to see a woman show sympathy for a suffering animal. Maybe it's a throwback to the time when he was a cave-dweller, tooth and claw against an enemy varmint, and his contrary female bet against him. Range hands laugh at sentiment. If they weren't born sadistic barbarians, they have become so by contemptuous familiarity. The Cowboy hit a tied-down calf across the nose with a hot branding iron because he was irritated by my remarks about his unnecessary cruelty.

The first fall that I undertook to brand my own cattle, there were some big spring calves with three-inch horns, most of them bulls. To say I had a tough time is understatement. To say I did it alone is false. I had a wonderful horse — man-trained, of course — to help me. We would get a long-ear into the corral and I would make a fire to heat the irons. After running the calf down afoot, I would snare the loop over his head and tie him to the fence. When I got a second rope around his hind legs above the hocks, I'd get on my good bay pony, Buddy, who would back up until the calf was stretched out. He would hold the taut rope while I got off, tied its front legs to the fence and loosened the neck rope before the calf strangled. While the struggling beast squirmed and fought I would call upon heaven in various ways, choked with smoke from burning hair, splattered with blood, gobs of black smear and dehorning paint. It was not an operation to be recommended.

One day I was working the country around some good corrals twelve miles from the nearest neighbor. Just as I arrived with a bunch of eight big unbranded calves, up rode three cowboys. I hailed them with joy. They were *puros vaqueros,* the McCoy of the craft. As one, the gallant three got off their horses and over the fence. Ropes swished and snapped home. In five minutes the eight calves were securely tied in the dust. But not even a fire built! As I scurried to rustle wood I thought of the tight tourniquets made by the thin *madrinas* (pigging strings) on all those legs, the circulation stopping, the crippling after effects! But I dared not open my mouth. They were experts; I was a woman.

One man started a blaze under the wood while the others took out their razor-sharp knives and went to work on the trussed-up animals. They got the squeezers and snipped off the horns. With no hot irons for cauterizing! Blood gushed and spouted and lay in thick puddles in the dirt.

I can never forget that hour of excessive, unusual, and — in truth — unnecessary gore. Left alone with the half-killed animals, I thought weakly: *"They meant to be kind. Kind to me."* Then I thought, with passionate fury, of how right was the literary wit who never wrote "mankind" but always "man-unkind."

Not counting experience and the printed word, the know-how (such as it is) that I have about maintaining

life and passable solvency in rough desert canyons stocked with cows, has been learned from men. My teachers could never have qualified for medals for patience or for courtesy. That's all right. I'm glad I was taught the hard way and had my head chewed off when I dallied in the pinches. Thereafter, when it was up to me to make good, if I couldn't get the job done, as the old saying goes; "two good men better not try."

CHAPTER 5

There Ought to be a Law

Sitting in a cattle growers' convention where, in round numbers, four hundred members were gathered, it came to me that I was in the midst of four hundred practicing physicians. This was only a small swatch of the world's vast array of livestock growers — all qualified doctors. By what right qualified? By the ancient right of ownership — the same that gave Cleopatra authority to try out her poisons and potions on her slaves. They were hers! Anyone who owns a four-legged creature is, *ipso facto*, privileged to dose it and practice surgery on it. For all practical purposes, a bill of sale or brand-inspection slip carries with it a veterinarian degree.

But it has occurred to me that maybe there ought to be a law prohibiting the practice of medicine by fools like us. The idea came to me while on all fours in the musty corners of the barn, hunting for black crickets to stew. My worry wasn't for the crickets. They died a merciful death when I snapped off their heads and dropped them into the saucepan. I pitied the dear horse out in the corral suffering the agonies of kidney colic. It is called that in range country. He could not void his bladder and was in terrible anguish, for a horse's pain is cut to size.

What effect the orthopterous brew might have was a mystery. I was shooting in the dark on the theory of "try anything once." Epsom salts and sweet spirits of nitre had not given relief. I had heard a cowman say he had cured a horse by inserting match heads, but that was too drastic for me. The dose of cricket broth had been recommended by the Old Vaquero, who now and then held the ranch on his shoulders but not at the time. I worked more in doubt than hope, and turned out to be right. Nothing resulted from the hard struggle with the horse but an added quart of liquid to his load.

Plagued by ignorance and helplessness, I jumped into the pickup and drove recklessly twelve miles to consult a friend who had spent a lifetime around horses.

"Oh, yes," he said confidently. "I kin tell you what to do. Git a bottle of turpentine" — he measured about two ounces with his hands — "and pour it on his back right exactly over his kidneys."

It sounded brutal to me, and again I was right. A blister like a saddle blanket spread across the poor horse's back. For that sin my penance was the expense and trouble of keeping him up and feeding him hay and grain while treating his burn with wet dressings of cold tea and boric acid. Fortunately the sturdy little horse recovered, and I learned a lesson. A better informed neighbor told me to remedy this affliction with Gold Medal Harlem Oil, and I have never been without it since, although years go by without the need for it.

Not too many years ago, the big sorrel I was keeping in the corral showed symptoms, and I made ready to dose him. Some miners were boarding with me temporarily while their accommodations were being built up the creek, so I took advantage of available manpower and asked for a volunteer. The three swing-shift men were lounging in the patio, and at a glance from the others, Lalo got up to go with me and hold the horse. As soon as he picked up a rope, I recognized him as a man of experience. Yes, he told me, he had worked on ranches down the Valley, and he ran a few head of his own on the Gila River. He wanted to know what I was pouring into the horse while he "eared" him down. I could see he wasn't impressed with my competence. Later I found out that when he came off shift at midnight, he got one of the boys to hold a flashlight for him, and he went down and "cured" my horse in his own way.

Cowboys of the old school have a simple faith in remedies they have learned by word of mouth: simple remedies, such as tying a hair tightly around the end bone in the horse's tail; or stuffing a wormy calf's navel with dry manure to stop blood and discourage flies. Whether it involves their own animals or the boss's, these cowhands are not squeamish about plying their primitive arts and sciences. You'll see one readily open his pocket-knife and slash a horse's nose to bleed him, or make a poultice of fresh cow manure to bind on an injury.

When the ranch "medic" finds a cow with a protruding vaginal passage, he ties her up and goes for the traditional *materia medica* — baling wire and a long-necked bottle. Sanitation is something new in range lore, and, to tell the truth, it doesn't seem to make much difference. The cowboy works with patient strength until he has pushed the cow's insides back into place. Then he inserts the bottle and sews her up with baling wire. In my part of rangeland, such cows are generally turned loose in this condition to take their chances. The bottle is supposed to keep them from straining inside-out again. Actually, it isn't the womb (as the cowmen call it) that protrudes, but the passage leading to it.

Usually the condition comes from a difficult birthing, but not always. My sister and I found a cow in bad shape three miles from the ranch, and drove her home on foot to take care of her. No bottle. And I used a sacking needle and strong twine. Then we went back to hunt the baby calf. We wore ourselves out with no success. The next day I turned her out and tried to follow her, hoping to save the baby. She went back to her grazing ground and ate for a couple of hours, then lay down in the shade — never once bawling or showing any sign of new motherhood. But cows are very foxy about hiding their young. As long as you are watching them, they will mosey around chewing on bushes, pretending to have not a care in the world when actually they are within a few yards of where they have hidden their young. When it was growing dark we gave up and came home. The next day we went back and found her contentedly grazing. This time I took a longer look at her udder and decided she was still expectant. We drove her to the corral again and shut her up. We had business in the city, but before we left, I put her in the chute and cut the twine. When we returned at midnight, I went down and found her lying comfortably in the moonlight with a big bull calf by her side.

With the first case of this kind that fell to me, I tried an improvement over the cowboy way. I stuffed the cow with sanitary napkins dipped in antiseptic solution, sewed her up with twine, and made a gunny-sack harness to steady the works instead of the bottle. She had been in extremely bad condition from long exposure and fly damage. I kept her in the corral — which meant a hay bill — and washed her twice daily with potassium permanganate solution. She became a member of the ranchhold, and I called her Old Kotex. My "daughter" Caroline, home over the weekend from the university, brought a boyfriend with her. As we walked up the hill to the corral, she begged me in a whisper not to mention Old "K" by name.

You may not have a natural bent or conscious desire

toward the medical profession, but if you enter the live-stock business you have medicine thrust upon you. The rancher must go farther and farther into back country looking for cheap grass and water, two commodities made increasingly rare by population density. Isolation throws him upon his own resources.

As of today, a membership such as that of our cattle growers' association will contain a sprinkling of graduates from animal husbandry classes. They are the ones who will think twice before opening their pocket-knives in the presence of a bloated cow; they will drive miles to get a vet's advice; and they are the biggest patrons of vet supplies.

And for modern vets the range of supplies available seems almost endless. Before the invention of medicated aerosol bombs, a kind neighbor brought his *vaquero* crew and helped me round up. When we got the long-ears in the corral for branding, I opened my drug closet and brought out — besides fly repellents, merthiolate and heal-ing powder for the castrations — ointment for the brands, blood stopper for the dehorning, and smear for wounds. The neighbor turned to his men, and forgetting that my Spanish is as good as his, murmured: "This woman is crazy about medicine."

I belong to the school of thought that declares: "Grease never cured nothin' on earth." Old Perry was with me in that. There was always a controversy between me and the Uncle, a grease man. When faced with abrasions, wounds, or swellings, he wanted to use mentholatum, tallow, snake oil. I held out for drying lotions — iodine, merthiolate, healing powder. While he was with me, we seldom had the advantage of expert advice, for vets were scarce, and money was scarcer. Even today, of the veterinarians in this area, centered in Tucson, five out of six practice only on small animals. If you can find one who will treat a cow or horse, it is no snap to take the sick one to town and keep it there the necessary length of time. We took a baby colt to a vet because it had a cactus spine broken off in its eyeball. The doctor was so interested he called some eye specialists, who came to his hospital and operated on the colt just for the experience. The colt got well, to our great satisfaction. When he got back to the ranch and found his mother in the corral waiting with plenty of warm milk, he was the happiest creature alive.

A young doctor, who had treated my dogs, was startled when I carried a three-week-old bull in my arms and laid him on the steel operating table of his small-animal hospital.

"What's that?" he asked hostilely.

"It's a small animal with pneumonia," I answered aggressively.

I explained that a schoolboy spending summer weeks on the ranch had found it at the bottom of the forty-foot cliff from which it had plunged. A palo verde tree had broken its fall, so that the only fractured bone was its lower jaw, where two teeth were missing. It had lain for hours exposed to the hot sun, and congestion had set in. I gave it canned milk with aspirin, a shot, and took it to town. The vet examined it with professional interest and concurred in my diagnosis.

"How much is this animal worth?" he asked, seeming to mean that it couldn't be much.

"It's not worth anything dead," I parried.

"Frankly," he said, "it would cost considerable money and a lot of trouble to cure."

His advice was that unless it would eventually bring a good sum, there was no use to make the investment. I understood that he was following the tenets of his profession by being honest with me. I did not feel capable of explaining to him that livestock owners are not always mercenary. Why did he think I had taken the two-hour drive to town with the calf's head on my lap, its hoarse breath in my ears? I was thinking of the calf's mother, of the months it had taken her to produce this nice little bull, of the bag of milk she had, and her broken heart if he died.

"Let's cure him," I said.

That was when antibiotics were very expensive. It cost $27 for the sulfa and penicillin, besides the office fee. It cost considerable money for the hay I had to feed the cow, while I milked her to pour the milk down the helpless calf via a soda pop bottle. Days passed before he could stand up, and a long time went by before his jaw healed enough for him to take food naturally. My time counted for something, especially while I was giving him the sulfa every four hours day and night. But, it was a thrill to see him live and grow and get fat. I called him Stevie for the fellow who leaped off Brooklyn Bridge. When he was a big yearling I got $100 for him. I don't know whether I made a profit or a loss on the deal, but I gained a victory.

Living a long way from the marts of trade, a rancher seldom has money in mind when tending to his stock, and probably needs cash more than do fellow citizens in town jobs. But other things count more, or ranches would be a thing of the past. When you cure a case of worms, you are saving a life. When an old cow comes in to water with a cholla knot sticking out on her jaw, and you get her into the chute, tie her head, sharpen your knife and plunge it in, trying to dodge the stream of "corruption" that shoots out, you're relieving the old cow's pain.

Once a cow staggered into the Windmill Ranch just as I happened along alone. She had a bone stuck in her throat which had prevented her from eating or drinking for several days. It was easy to push her over and tie her legs. I thrust a smooth sahuaro rib into her mouth so she couldn't bite me, rammed my hand down her throat, and jerked out the bone. Then I tried for two hours to get her up. I even made a tripod of poles over her and tried to pull her up with ropes. She would not make the slightest effort. Gratefully she swallowed the water I poured down her, but she wouldn't eat any hay. Her torture had been too cruel. She quit.

Nothing dies as willingly as a cow. If things are favorable she goes along placidly functioning day by day, but at heart she doesn't care a great deal about living. When the going is tough, she gives up. When she lies down to die, she wants no interference.

Perhaps it's the indifferent lack of cooperation that gives you a feeling of uplift when you bring a doomed one back to life. It was a big thrill to save Old Frenchie's life soon after her last calf was born.

The Nephew and I arrived home with a load of hay about nine-thirty one night and found a message from the people at the mine that a cow was sick and probably dying up at the fork of the canyons. We hurried the two miles to see what cow it was, what ailed her, what could be done about it, and if there was a little calf that could be saved. Old Frenchie lay in complete collapse, able to move only her eyelids. She had a young calf poking around in the bushes at the edge of the tailings dump where she had fallen. It looked hopeless. I had a gun ready if worse came to worst; Nephew said later he had a speech all ready, begging me not to shoot her.

It was a case of poison. That much I knew. From there, I ran up against the wall of ignorance that has plagued me always in my role of Florence Nightingale to the bovines. Unable to figure out what had caused the poisoning, I gave her the full therapy at my command. We made three round trips up the canyon that night. I will never know if it was the quart of mineral oil, the pint of Pepto-Bismol, or the 10 cc's of penicillin that gave her a boost. By morning, she still breathed and had managed to turn around. We hooked the jeep to her hind legs and pulled her out of the hollow she was in, dangerously close to a machine-made ditch, and got her across the tailings dam to some bushes where she could have shade. I repeated my dosing and poured several bottles of water down her throat. We scattered soft alfalfa for a pillow, rigged up some gunny-sacks to help shut out the hot sun, and went off, miles away, to work. On one of our trips down the canyon the night before, we had taken the little calf home and put him on another cow, feeling certain that he would never see his mother again.

After a long day that lasted till dark, we took the flash-lights and our medical paraphernalia, some hay and water, and drove up to see our patient. Nephew went up alone to the top of the dam. "If she's alive," I said, "wave your light and I'll climb the steep slope with the jeep." As I waited, I thought sadly of what a good thrifty cow she had been; faithfully furnishing the outfit with a nice fat calf each year.

At the signal I threw the jeep into granny-gear and mounted the dam. There was Frenchie, two hundred yards from where we had left her, sitting up cow-fashion under a mesquite. She got up and drank water out of the pail, but we had to tie her to the tree to give her the injection. I was shaken by the miracle of her survival. She had been found just in time. And we had happened to hit on the right cure. Next day she walked the two miles down to the corrals and went about the business of recovering and of raising her calf.

Bum Ears was a steer who was orphaned at birth; and that statement only begins his sad story. He was born in the shipping pens at the railroad, almost at the moment his mother was hustled up the chute and into the car to go to summer pasture up north. He would have been trampled to death in the crowded railroad car. The two men who had bought the cows came back to knock the wet sprawling baby in the head. Like Pocahontas, I threw myself between him and the fence post that was to give him the *coup de grâce*.

"You can't raise that thing," the old Cowman argued. "Without a drop of his mother's milk he won't get along. No matter what you feed him, he'll take sick and die."

But he wiped the calf off with a gunnysack and put him on the car seat beside me for the fifty-mile journey. He did take sick, but I wouldn't let him die. For a long time he wavered up and down, so that every morning I ran to the barn to see if he was still breathing. At last, nursing care prevailed. And finally I persuaded the milk cow to raise him with her own calf. It wasn't easy to do. Every time she kicked at him, I kicked her; and it happened that my endurance outlasted hers.

But for all the trouble and care, the poor calf didn't thrive. His misery came to a focal point in his ears, which both ran malodorously with canker sores. Each morning I carried a fountain syringe and tube up to the corral and washed out his ears with warm boric-acid water, then filled them with healing powder. They were still sore when he was a yearling — and still sore when he was two. On account of his affliction, we didn't dehorn him. As shipping time after shipping time went by with Bum Ears in no condition to go, the Uncle said: "We'll keep him for his horns. When they git five or six feet spread, somebody'll buy him for a set of longhorns."

Bum Ears was coming four years old when I took him down to an extraordinarily smart cowboy, who tied him down and injected a pint of sodium iodide into his jugular vein. And lo, he was cured. After years of my practical nursing, as if from a miracle, Bum Ears was a well steer. In the spring he weighed nearly a thousand pounds.

Yesterday I rode by the place I call the Bone Yard — a flat point overlooking the deep canyon — where I drag off the remains of my mistakes. When I pass there, I am confronted by the bones of the wretched ones who lost out on my blind gamble of cure-or-kill. For all my good intentions, they died from my ignorance, or my negligence in not finding them in time. I dread to think of the animals that perish each day because of such human frailties. Cattle people cannot spend years in the study and research necessary for medical proficiency. We must go on guessing.

The most onerous thing about range doctoring, particularly in my case, is that it must be done by a combat of strength. You get nothing from the patient but contrary opposition. A range cow's instinct tells her that people are no good, and her first aim is to stay as far away from them as she can.

Minorities, avalanched under by centuries of despair, have a tendency to work up to the surface of human consciences. After millions of years (nineteen, is it?), women have done so over most of the world. Then children. And the aged. And the poor. And the variously-pigmented. Everywhere the oppressed are heaving mightily against the weight of misery.

After people come the animals.

Already, dogs have come a good way out of their doom of suffering, as have cats. In all urban communities there are small-animal hospitals competently equipped and staffed. Few families, of whatever economic status, fail to take their pets in a health crisis to a doctor.

Not long ago I read of a plan, in St. Louis it was, promoting hospital insurance for dogs. Perhaps the idea will spread.

With large beasts such as cows, the story is not so good. They have no declaration of rights. Nobody loves them. They are means, not ends; not so much living creatures as negotiable wealth — "money on four legs." What hygienic service they get is done for the sake of making a dollar for the owner.

But there is revolution abroad in the matter of animal care. An increasing number of veterinarians in every state make it their concern to promote the life and health of large animals. Federally endowed scientists have made wonderful contributions — in chemistry and allied subjects — to the welfare of livestock during the time I have been ranching. Cattle associations sponsor ranch schools at least once a year where members can ask questions of experts and see the vets in action.

The law I've been thinking about is on its way. Time will come when an ignoramus like me, who starts out with a razor-sharp knife to operate on some trussed-up animal, will have to keep an eye out for enforcement officers of a law prohibiting all but properly certified persons from practicing medicine beyond the common measures of first aid.

Speaking for those under my care, I say: *Speed the day!*

CHAPTER 6

To Market

> Oh, we rounded them up and put them
>   on the cars,
> And that was the last of the 2U-Bars

sang the cowpunchers who followed the Chisholm Trail.
But that quick summary wasn't the half of it. The hun-
dred-odd verses in the old song — whatever version you
hear — tell about hungry days and sleepless nights, blizzards, hailstorms, stampedes, dry runs . . .

> He jumped in the saddle and gave a little yell,
> And the swing cattle broke and the leaders went
>   to hell.
> And the boss came around with a cutter in his
>   hand
> And swore he'd fire every Dad-Blamed man . . .

There was trouble, worlds of trouble, shipping cattle
to market in the old days. There still is.

Mine began with my first shipment in a downright
unusual way. Cattle trucks had come into use by that time,
so I only had to trail the calves — and their mothers, for
no human being can drive calves just taken off the cows —
a couple of miles down the canyon to some old corrals
and make a temporary loading chute out of fence posts
and brush.

I had thirteen calves to go. Eleven weighed no more than 400 pounds each and sold for three cents a pound. The two that weighed 500 went at two and a half cents a pound.

We put up a makeshift chute which the worried cattle tore down a few times before we got the calves separated from the mothers and loaded into the bobtail truck sent out by the buyer. They were white-faces, fat and pretty. I was proud of them, and still remember being touched by the pathetic way they peered back at me as I followed their truck in my little Model A.

At a little more than half the distance we had to go, we rimmed the outskirts of the city to take a main highway westward. Just as we were passing the cemetery gate five miles from town, a car ignored a stop sign and dashed out from a side road. The truck driver swerved, the wheels struck a soft shoulder bordering a deep ditch, and the truck flipped over on its side, spilling out my calf crop. Without the slightest hesitation, the liberated weaners jumped the low hedge and began eating the grass on the tree-shaded graves. The caretaker, armed with a hoe, ran over shouting and laying about, demanding that we get "them cows" out of his cemetery. The driver and I blocked his efforts to chase them out into the highway traffic, and our whoops, whistles, and cow-country antics won the day. The calves romped over the turf of the opulent graves, knocked down a few markers on the bare mounds identifying the cheaper plots, and escaped into the mesquite thicket on the uncleared area at the back of the huge burial grounds.

I went to hunt a telephone. My friend Baylor, the cattle inspector, who had spent a lifetime on Texas and New Mexico rangelands, had told me to call him when I reached the junction of the highways, and he would come out to inspect the calves to save taking them on into town through the heavy traffic. He heard my wild story and finally believed it.

"Ain't this a Friday?" he asked. It was.

"Well, I vow," he teased. "You can't expect me to have nothing to do with thirteen calves on a Friday in a graveyard. No Ma'am!"

He harped on this theme until he almost had me thinking he was serious.

Before I got back to the scene of disaster, a big wind had come up from the south. By the time the inspector arrived, a great dust storm obscured the view in every direction. The inspector offered to call in a couple of young fellows in the vicinity who kept horses, but horsemen were useless in the thicket of second-growth mesquite — the thorniest branch that grows. I went in afoot to scare out the calves. Being in my ladylike town clothes, my silk stockings and print crepe dress were ripped and threaded in the thorny maze, and later on, soaked, when a heavy shower overtook us in the lane leading to the slaughter house where we borrowed a chute to reload our cattle. The driver had called a wrecker to come out and help him right the bobtail, which had received only minor injuries besides losing all its oil.

It was long after dark when we got to the buyer's corrals near Red Rock; he had to write my check by car lights. No telling how many pounds the calves had shrunk on their long day's journey, but I was kidded about turning them into the cemetery lawn to put a fill on them.

That episode started my shipping troubles. And more recent events have proved that it was only the beginning. I took a couple of long yearling steers, one weighing 650 pounds and the other 730, to the livestock auction in my pickup, topping the season with my best calves. Nothing unusual marred the trip, but I didn't get to stay to see my steers sold. I had to go looking for a little lost calf.

A neighbor had kindly offered to haul a cow I called Wild Bill in his big cattle truck with some of his own he said were as wild as she was. That was a real favor. Wild Bill was an old cow with tiger blood in her veins, a real live one-horned people-hater. Horseback, I could drive her to the ranch corrals with a little bunch of her less savage pals, but the minute she found herself in durance vile she made sure no human being went in with her. That made it impossible for me to put her in the crowding chute for loading. Even if I had been able to load her into the pickup, she surely would have torn the wooden rack apart with her bare horns. It was really a stroke of luck when my neighbor's men drove her to his ranch with some of his cows that had strayed into my country. From there he could take her to town, when he had gathered a load of his own, in his big truck that was supposed to be cow-proof.

I welcomed a chance to get rid of her without having to shoot her. She was born wild. Her mother was a big, reasonably gentle cow named Pennsylvania. But Wild Bill took to the hills at sight of a human being from the time she was a calf. The only reason I kept her was that I could never catch her to sell when she was a yearling. When she was six years old she hurt a front foot between the toes and flies got in. We tracked her by the blood on the rocks in the rough canyon she occupied. With a little bunch of well-behaved cows we got her to the corrals. She could jump out of all — except the hospital one made of solid mesquite poles. Fortunately she liked hay. The only way I could cure her foot was by dropping a flake of hay into her corral against her side of the fence, then lying flat on the ground on my side so she couldn't see me, when she edged up to eat, I'd reach under the bottom pole with a long stick ending in a swab of worm medicine, and give her wound a good swipe before she dashed away.

It was sometime before my neighbor was ready to take her away. When one day I met him at the post office, he told me Wild Bill had had a calf. Half-heartedly, I offered to bring her home. No, he said, he would wait a few days until the calf was strong enough to go, and she would bring more money with the baby by her side.

At the auction ring that Saturday I settled myself in a good spot, anticipating seeing poor old frightened Wild Bill put the arena directors behind the barriers or on the fence. Then in came my neighbor with a long face and told me he had lost her calf on the way to town. There was a hole in his wooden rack, and the little one had evidently found it and fallen out. He didn't know it until he arrived at the stock yards to unload. It was fifty miles back to Mammoth where he had made his last stop.

I signalled the Nephew and back we went in the middle of the hot July day, driving slowly as he scanned the right side of the highway, and I the left. My hope was to find a little dead body; then I wouldn't have to lie awake thinking about the lost baby slowly starving to death as it wandered through the heat and cactus. Nephew's hope was to find it alive, for if we did it would be his.

Our search was unsuccessful. We kept looking as we suffered the heat on the slow drive back to town to pick up the check for the steers. However, the story had a happy ending. That night my neighbor found the baby calf not far from his ranch corrals where it had been loaded. I went next morning and brought it home. And, by good luck, for it doesn't happen too often, I got it adopted by a young cow who had given birth to a stillborn calf.

Moving livestock is never easy and often hazardous. Gathering and shipping often breeds crises. Some *body* is going to be hurt; sometimes a man's, more often an animal's. After a "work," the horses are bunged up. Some are crippled for life. Cattle suffering is inevitable. Cattle locate in certain areas which they claim as their own. To drive them out is like driving refugees from their lifetime homes before an invading enemy. For the weaners — the calves to be sold — it is the end of their good, free life on the range; never again will they know the warm comfort of a milk-giving mother ready to defend them with her life. For days after they are taken away, the ranch is loud with bovine cries of anxiety and bereavement.

The accidents are of various kinds. One time we had brought in nine big steers, all in heavy enough condition to mash the scales, and every pound needed to pay the bank. Next morning we found that one had been shoved into the manger upside down. He was dead, with his feet sticking up in the air and his body so swollen the Uncle had to get a block and tackle to dislodge him. I had a weary time chasing his mother two miles down the canyon and across a fence, so she wouldn't have to see the cadaver of her son dragged off to the bone pile.

One year we had a steer with peculiar white lines down his back and across his shoulders and front legs. We called him Pinto. He ranged over at the Big Tank, eight miles from headquarters. As I drove him in, fat and slick, he was a sight to catch the eye. It was nearly dark and I had a little trouble penning my bunch. Next morning, as we drove our yearlings to a neighbor's shipping pen, we noticed something was wrong with Pinto. He stuck his neck far out, led with his nose, and walked in a way to show distress. By the time we reached the corrals it was obvious he was sick; the buyer cut him back. He was able to stagger the two miles back to the ranch before collapsing. Large doses of salts and mineral oil did not help.

When the Uncle dragged his dead body over into the Bone Yard next morning, I followed with a sharp knife and an axe, determined to perform an autopsy to see what was the cause of death. The Uncle was against it. He would have nothing to do with it. He argued that I might get dangerous corruption on my hands and take "colery-morbus" or some such foul thing. My smidgen of science stood by me. Search revealed in his first stomach a long strip of red inner tube that had been used to wrap a broken pipe near the corral. The university laboratory confirmed this as the killer of poor Pinto.

Before the local livestock auctions came into being, it was a headache to find some truck to haul the cattle after the trouble of hunting a buyer to get a delivery contract. For several years I shipped to, or by, or with old T.C., the most famous (some have said infamous) cattle buyer in our parts. The advantages were that he would buy my cattle at *some* price, no matter how slow the market, and, to my amazement, he would give a woman who had no business being in the cow industry practically the same price per pound or by the head that he gave big operators. Besides, he owned — or controlled — his own trucks.

"How many you got?" he would shout into the telephone at six o'clock in the morning, about the only hour I could contact him.

Then he would say, "Get them up to the Green House corrals, and I'll buy them if anybody can."

When asked what he would give, he never hemmed and hawed. He came right out with his price. We — and here I crossed my fingers — would agree on a day and hour for delivery, and I would drive home wishfully thinking that *this* time maybe T.C. would keep the appointment. As the seasons rolled by, my hopes dimmed. There was never any telling when he or his trucks would show up.

The Uncle, the Old Vaquero, and I would be up bright and early. We were never once late with our cattle. We would shut them up in the shipping pen, unsaddle, tie our horses in the shade, and try to find a bearable place in which to lie down and fight ants and flies while waiting. Usually the hour was supposed to be ten o'clock, as it took the trucks two hours to come from town. Eleven o'clock would come. And twelve. I would break out the sandwiches and fruit. The long afternoon would drag on. At four or five the men would give up and go home to do the chores. I would turn the cattle out into the little holding pasture and catch a ride to the village to call T.C.'s wife. She would tell me, innocently enough, that he had gone to Nogales that day to receive 500 steers; or to Phoenix with two truckloads of cows. When he got a bigger deal than ours, he forgot about us.

And sometimes when he made an effort to be there, his old trucks would break down. During the war years they ran on their reputation, as whose motor vehicles didn't? But when he began making money in five or six figures, he still would buy my little bunch, although he had ever less compunction about standing me up if a better opportunity offered. He merely laughed and joked and teased about leaving me in the lurch. My misery did have lots of company. All over the countryside, especially among family-sized ranches, cussing old T.C. was a main topic at any gathering.

After I weighed them out to him on a neighbor's scales, I still had to be uneasy about the cattle. But at least the responsibility and the loss were now his, not mine. Once a load of my good steers sat all day in the heat in a dip on the mountain road while the driver caught a ride to town and brought out parts and a mechanic. There was a very steep hill three miles from the village where the paved highway began. Only a truck in number-one working order could make it without help. Otherwise one semi would unhook its trailer and hitch on to help the other up the grade. The cattle all piled into the back end of the rack and didn't always come out the same. A neighbor pulling a load of cows up that long hill killed five of them in that manner. Space was at a premium; they were packed in like sardines. Some were knocked down and trampled. Most drivers would stop and try to get them up. But not all. Some of old T.C.'s drivers, exhausted from lack of sleep and over-exertion, perhaps irritated at not getting their pay on time, or not getting their trucks repaired, would stop along the road for a few beers, letting the cattle shrink. I always followed the cattle if they were to be weighed in town, as was the case when T.C. got his own yards and scales.

Even with arrival at the city stockyards, we still didn't have it made. One time a bunch of my yearlings undertook to go down the unloading chute all at the same time when they were released from the truck. A board was knocked off the chute, and the last yearling — a wild one from the cholla flats farthest from the ranch corrals — jumped out and hit the ground running like a scared rabbit. There was no outside fence to stop him. I took after the steer in my little Ford, realizing that he could cut corners that I couldn't, but knowing nothing else to do in the split second it happened. He ran across vacant lots and over deep ditches and hit the old unfashionable part of town at a high trot. As I hurried through the narrow dirt streets, I could catch glimpses of his bobbing rump now and then, or see a clump of children gaping in wonder. *"¡Mira la vaca!"* (Look at the cow!) they cried.

Before he reached the paved streets, reinforcement came in the form of a young friend from the East who belonged to a roping club and was keeping his horse in T.C.'s yards. He took after the steer on his thousand-dollar pony, and I managed to stay close enough to tell, by the confusion and animation among the populace, which way they went. Right through the big city center they sped, disregarding traffic and traffic lights, crossing at a busy five-points, heading east. When at last I caught up, about six or eight miles from the pens, Dave Stout had roped the heaving steer in an opening cleared for a housing project. I went back for help. Someone had a pickup with a horse trailer. About dark we hauled the fugitive back to his fat hay-munching buddies in the stockyards. And to this day I hold it against old T.C. that when we weighed the runaway, not one pound was allowed for all that shrinkage. I offered the gallant young man who had saved my calf ten dollars, but he settled for a drink on old T.C., not having learned to be western about livestock.

The worst shipping jam I ever got into was the time I delivered eighty cows, about twenty of them with calves, at a town down on the Gila River at the end of a railroad spur. I had known the little town only as a place the highway passed through. I had no idea how non-up-to-date it was as a shipping point.

Another bad year had struck Arizona. There was no spring feed, and the cow market dropped out of sight. I had put this little bunch on an irrigated alfalfa field on the river and hoped to keep them there for ninety days. Somebody will always buy cattle if they are fat. Then, before it was too late, it rained in West Texas and made a surplus of green stuff needing cows to eat it.

I was doctoring some cattle for pinkeye in a corral on the farm where the cows were pastured when a car drew up, and over the fence crawled a Texas buyer, full of business. He sized up the cows and their owner, and dived into his buying routine, not in the least interested in whether or not I was sincere in saying I was not ready to sell. After a certain amount of dickering he cornered me into saying I would take $80 for the dry cows and $110 for the pairs. But what I really wanted was to keep the cows until they were fat. For my firmness he got even with me, although I did not realize it at the time, by writing into the contract where the cows were to be delivered to the railroad. I scarcely noticed the clause. The point was only thirty-two miles away, and I did not dream there was a place on any railroad in the world where trucks couldn't get to the loading pens.

For once, I was not worried about shrinkage, and for once the trucks came on time. The Old Vaquero and I rode with the drivers of the semis while the Uncle went in my car, chauffeured by the Star Boarder. They brought the lunches and coffee pot. Not until my driver turned off the highway to private stockyards this side of the river did I wake up to my problem. Across the river and the other side of town, (a full mile and a half from our present location) the railroad loading pens perched on a rough hillside, beside tracks laid on a rocky cut high above the paved highway. There was no access road a truck could maneuver, leaving no way in the world to get the cattle up to the pens except to walk them. The train was ordered. We were miles from our horses. And the agent sent to receive the cows told me he would give me my check only when the cattle were counted out in the railroad stock pens.

The owner of the corrals where we had unloaded and watered suggested that I go to town and look in a certain bar where I might find Don Antonio, a rancher who had also brought cows to go to the Texas buyer. His ranch was near. He had driven his cattle in early, put them in corrals adjacent to those we were using, and had gone with all his *vaqueros* to the town's cold spot to wait out the heat of the day. I didn't like the idea of joining forces, uninvited, with a stranger. It amounted to throwing myself on his mercy. There was not room in the railroad pens for both bunches of cows, and they had to be received and counted separately. Mine should be out of the way and on the cars before Don Antonio was ready.

The May weather was firecracker-hot in the river bottom. Don Antonio was an old man, but this handicap was offset by bold manly grit. It was plain that he had occupied his bar stool for hours and was keeping right up with his rough cowpunchers, can for can.

Seguro que si! (of course!) he would help a woman get her cows to the yards. Of course he would lend me his horse, his own personal mount. But the day "made hot." The heat was bad for the cows. Bad for the horses. Bad for the peoples. "Give her beer!" he shouted, finding a stool for me, stating that we would await a fresh hour in which to move cows.

Gallant Don Antonio! He will always occupy a bright page in my memory for the quick answer he gave when I asked the question that had always perplexed and tormented me: What to do with your cherished horses when they get old? Without a moment's hesitation his answer came straight and sure: "I feed them hay and grain." *Bravo,* Don Antonio! *Olé, olé, olé!*

I regretted that Fate had not cut me out to excel in tact or in the consumption of the refreshments served in cool, dark, music-jangled bars. And rejoiced that I was soon able to convince my host that all my troubles were from the lack of a horse.

The Uncle and the Old Vaquero, lying in the shade, enduring heat and flies, eyed me with disgust. I had been gone longer than they could see any excuse for. But I had a horse! Only one, to be sure, but one that knew his business. When the Old Vaquero was up on him, he forgot his pique and took to the cows like three men. The Uncle, more forgiving every step that brought him nearer the cool bar, helped me bring up the drags afoot. In all his life, he remarked, this was the first time he had made a cattle drive afoot — and using a walking cane to boot!

We had a delicate job. Most of our cows were gentle, but there were several from the *chollales* as wild as lizards. None of them had ever walked the streets of a town, or seen street traffic, or crossed a concrete bridge over a river. The road approaching the bridge was not fenced, but cut through thick mesquite and *batamote* clumps. The credit for not losing a cow must go to the Uncle's habit of using nothing but paper money. His town pants hung heavy with coins. We had no more than got a good start when a swarm of boys appeared, and they were fast to respond to the Uncle's method. When an old cow sneaked off into the brush he would cry: "Put her back, kid!" The boy who put her back got a dime or a nickel or a quarter — whatever came first to hand.

It would have been easy to lose the whole bunch when we crossed the bridge and turned into Main Street. Fortunately, there were folks who saw our predicament and held up the cars until we passed. The Uncle's shouts and my whistles apparently reassured our uneasy cattle, and long before dark (and before Don Antonio considered the hour propitious for his drive), we counted out every cow to the agent.

Now that there is the convenience of weekly livestock auction sales, shipping need not be such a hazard. You can have your own small truck and take the animals to town two or three at a time. But you never can be sure of anything about delivering cattle until you have your check.

I had three yearlings to take one Saturday, and stopped in the village to hunt the cattle inspector to get papers on them. I parked in front of his office and stepped across the street to see if he were having his breakfast in the café, when a passer-by boogered the cattle. A big quarter-Brahma steer jumped on the endgate and broke it down. Away went the yearlings around the sheriff's office and off to hunt for home. In a second I was in the pickup, rushing to see which way they had disappeared.

As I roared around the corner, help arrived in the form of two young miners, just off graveyard shift, who had seen the escape. They were country boys who had some horses pastured across the river on a farm. The horses were loose in the field, and it took some time to drive them to the corral, saddle them, and ride back to the lane where I held the steers. I had met the vagrants just as they were backing up to make a running broad jump over the obstructing cattleguard. A whoop and a rock turned them back, and I drove madly to beat them to the other end of the lane — entrance to the wide river bed. There I again attacked them with rocks, and back they scurried toward the cattleguard, where I arrived just in time to turn them again. Thus we played pussy-wants-a-corner for what seemed to me a full hour before the two horsemen arrived and drove the played-out yearlings to a local corral and helped me reload them.

This adventure, though not disastrous, put a good big shrink on my steers, well counterbalancing the bait of hay I had fed them that morning.

With shipping, no matter how well planned, there is always the chance of a crisis. It used to be nightguards and blizzards and stampedes. Now it can be broken-down trucks, delayed trains, holes in fences or truck-racks, and men and animals on the prod. Among the cattle, you will always find Fiery and Snuffy. Among the horses there'll be some salty jugheads. And men? If the work lasts long enough, there'll be gripes and peeves which can fester into cussings and fist-fights.

If it has to do with livestock, there is no such thing as a cinch.

CHAPTER 7

Beware the Buyer

Centuries ago, when barter was evolving into commerce, the trade policy was summed up as *caveat emptor,* let the buyer beware. It was his own fault if the purchaser ended the deal with a balky horse or a barren cow. In general, dealers considered it respectable — even admirable — to cheat the customer. So what did the buyers do to turn the tables? The smart ones began moving westward, and the farther west they went, the smarter they grew. By the time they hit the American range country the boot was entirely on the other foot, and buyers were the terror of the industry.

Through the cold of winter and dry famine of summer you fought from daylight till dark to keep the calf crop alive and thriving. You mortgaged the future to feed your little bunch. You drew on all your strength and endurance to protect your cattle from disease and pests. When they reached their prime, you put forth limitless effort to gather them and provide a good holding place. Then came the climax: finding a buyer, one fair enough to allow you to appease creditors and stay in the business.

No matter how affable a fellow you met, the minute you propositioned him to buy your cattle, he shed honor and generosity as he would his coat if preparing to wrestle. It was immediate "king's excuse" from friendship — or even kinship. He might have been your brother-in-law, or maybe, since you were a woman, your suitor. No matter. If he considered buying livestock, his whole mind was on getting the bottom dollar.

Now, in the more civilized present, when I find myself in a bind for money, happily I think of the weekly livestock auction and my spirit lifts, if not to heaven's gate, at least upwards to bold bright self-confidence. No more cowering and fawning and half-hearted haggling. Any week the financial going gets tough, I throw the rack on the pickup, load on a cow, or two or three head of young stuff too fat to merit keeping or too poor to make the weather hazards, and off I go, sure of a pleasant welcome from the sale operators who at times go so far as to compliment me on the condition of my cattle. What old cattle buyer ever did that!

I sit in dignity — if not comfort — on the hard bench and watch the bidders go as high for my cattle as they do for anybody else's of like quality. Whatever cutting back is done comes naturally, not as a personal penalty for being a poor bargainer or a member of the needier sex. No cause to burn with shame and resentment when an animal bearing my brand fails to make top grade. Nobody sneers because my calf has too much white on his back, or too little width to his skull. The bidders may sit on their hands but at least they don't gloat over me in person. I don't have to be party-of-the-second-part to humiliating arguments and niggling disputes. Both sides can relax in decent silence.

Oh, yes, I know what goes on. The auction, after all, is a human concern; of people, by people, for people. And if there ever is a time when people are excessively human, it is when money is involved — especially in a livestock trade. At slack times most of the buyers at an auction are local butchers and packers. If there is a shortage of cattle, they may go so far as to bid against each other seriously. But in a world where things are as they are rather than as they should be, competitive bidding on livestock is sometimes less than reality. I sat behind a row of buyers one afternoon and restrained an impulse to clop one over the head with my loaded handbag. My good old cow was being switched around in the ring and the auctioneer was getting some lively response. Then this fellow leaned across his neighbors to shut up his rival by saying: "I let you have that bull. Now gimme the cow!"

At slow times when there is no out-of-town competition, there is a maddening (to the seller) kind of buddyism in the bidding. "Let's stay under twenty today," you seem to hear them saying. Or, "Them ole *shelly* cows orten to bring mor'n six-eight cents."

When range feed is in sight (the desert blooming with the lush green and lavender filaree) cattle are hard to come by and auctions fulfill their avowed purpose of offering an open market. Prosperity is in the air, keyed up to the clatter of the spieler and the yelps of the ring men. Your cattle have as good a chance as the next one's, and you needn't worry because salesmanship was left out of your make-up.

But never, never, can you lean back with a comfortable feeling that you have it made. The human error factor pops up at auctions behind the scenes, and it has a special sting. If you sell directly to a buyer, your bollixes are your own fault, and maybe you can learn a lesson. At a busy animal mart, you are at the mercy of other people's foul-ups.

I still burn at the memory of what happened to Old Strawberry, a good, big cow who had been a pillar of the little place for years. She was fat and had a good steer calf by her side. Arriving at the unloading chute at ten-thirty,

I felt relieved to think I'd get through early and be home before dark. At the afternoon auction they receive cattle until twelve noon. In the semi unloading just ahead of me, I spotted a tall yellow Brahma cow, noting mentally that I could look for my cow to be sold soon after that one went through the ring. It happened to be a big day. Time wore on to three o'clock before the yellow Brahma came through.. Now, thought I, my turn next. But no. More and more cows were turned in — scores of them. One outfit had sent in sixty-five cows, and they were passed through the arena one at a time. Hours passed. The crowd thinned. The number of buyers lessened as quotas were filled. Still no Strawberry. Five o'clock, the usual closing time, came and passed. They began running through the lame and the halt and the blind. The only bidders left were those looking for scrubs, the pitiful ones that are "given away." At five-thirty, to an empty house, the last two head were shoved in; Old Strawberry and her calf, having shrunk all day in the small shadeless pen without water. The hurt remains yet, though I never knew who goofed, for I never went there again.

I didn't have to. For there is a morning auction across town on the same day. Naturally, it has an earlier deadline. Doomed by sex to house and yard chores and not always fortunate enough to have more corral hands than my own, and being obliged, part way on my journey, to make contact with a livestock inspector whose duties and activities are not confined to his office, I am often not quite under the wire. There has grown up a joke, a neighbor told me, around the sales place. When they see me backing up to the deserted unloading chute they say: "Here's that little green truck. Now we can begin the sale."

They are friendly people, favoring me with patience. But, alas, a worm lurks at the core of even this golden apple. Once I arrived with three nice yearlings, one of them not weaned, after the curtain had gone up. My twelve-year-old boy-companion Preston was sent in to ask one of the brothers in charge if we were too late. The one I know better came out himself to help me unload and tag my cattle. Relieved and appreciative, I went in and sat on a lower bench to watch the sale. I saw all the cows and calves and bulls and yearlings go through the ring — all except mine — saw the crowd rise to go, and heard the auctioneer say: "See you next Saturday, folks."

I got up and stood by the railing until my friend saw me. He was covered with embarrassment. He had shoved my yearlings into an out-of-the-way pen and forgotten them. "Leave them here," he insisted, "I'll feed them good and sell them next week. Won't cost you anything."

The little steer, just cut away from his mother, would lose weight and some hireling would or would not feed them right; but there was nothing else to do. As he had promised, next week the steers were sold, and I received a check with nothing deducted for feed. Months later I sent in some calves by the Nephew. From the check given to him, there had been deducted the feed bill for the yearlings sold in the spring. Perhaps the other brother took a more profit-wise view of the affair. Or some vigilant bookkeeper may have saved the old slip all summer to wait for my next shipment. In commerce as in war, somebody is going to get hurt.

There are several chances that you take. Modern gadgetry and equipment — all such facilities — are made for machines, not animals. The approach to the auction corrals is arranged for the convenience of trucks, not cattle. To unload, you do not drive into an enclosed area where your livestock may be secure: you back up to a platform wide-open to the street and take your chances passing frightened animals across and into the corral chute. At times, only a town youngster or two is available to man the unloading gates. Occasionally a wild cow or Brahma bull gets away and makes headlines by trampling an innocent bystander, or by showing off the roping and riding skills of the local peace officers. Slow one morning getting around to the back of my pickup where I had placed it at the platform, I was stunned to see that two youngsters assigned to the job had untied the endgate of the truck and jerked it out — without remembering to swing open the guard rails from truck to chute. There on the landing stood my two steers with nothing between them and the North Star but a four-foot drop and a city full of traffic and domiciles. When I complained later to the proprietor, he said, shaking his head: "You can't get no help these days." Fortunately, my calves were gentle ones raised around the home corral, and they waited patiently to be taken care of. Only one time, over the decades, have I lost an animal while unloading.

Whatever the hazards, I'm still all in favor of auctions. So, I should think, would be any small rancher who was around in the old days, when buyers were autocrats and had to be handled. What old-timer does not sigh when he thinks of trying to sell cattle back in the Thirties, and farther back? When his cattle were gathered, he put on his best clothes and went out to hunt a buyer. He haunted hotel lobbies and stockyards — beating around the bush when talking to other ranchers, for in those days if you found a good buyer, you held him close to your chest like a winning poker hand. In case a generous neighbor or pure luck put you next to one, you hurried home, got up a few of the best ones for a sample, and waited for the buyer to come out and make a trade.

Often when the buyer came to see the cattle, he brought

along an experienced commission man; or, if a commission man himself, his backer. Usually the woman of the ranch had fixed a good dinner or made a lemon pie or whatever was her specialty. But until the trading was done, the cold-fish buyers would have nothing but water — or maybe coffee. They would make no commitment to sociability.

The weaners or steers or mixed yearlings were bunched in the smallest corral to make them look bigger and more uniform; also to give less chance for individual inspection. The mother cows left bawling outside the corral were good ones. The *corrientes* (the mediocre) had been shunted off out of sight at dawn. The buyers must get the impression the herd was of high quality.

When the personnel involved arrived at the corral, the cattle were stared at a while in silence, the buyer then and there making up his mind and his argument. The companion of the buyer climbed up on the fence out of the way, but within helping range. The henchmen of the seller found jobs around close, just to be handy. There was no knowing what might happen when the parties of the first and second parts got down on their hunkers with sharpened wits and whittling knives and joined in the most cold-hearted contest of wills ever known to man: that of getting ahead of the other fellow in a trade.

To this day, I am touched by the anguish I endured on a black morning in the last months of the depression when I first crossed swords with a cattle buyer all by myself. My banker, who was also his banker and on a much larger scale, had sent this trader out to look at my spring "harvest." I had sixteen heifers and twenty steers corraled in a neighbor's little shipping pen on the highway two miles — no road — from my place. Having done some research, I had made up my mind to get six cents for the heifers and seven for the steers. My undoing was that I was silly enough to come right out and name my figures on the first go-round — a deadly mistake in the game of trading.

The buyer, a tall, dark, prosperous-looking man, came early, at eight o'clock on the dot, bringing with him his tall, dark, prosperous-looking wife — making the odds two to one at the start. The moment they looked at me (and this is a fact) they positively beamed at each other — an easy mark!

Of course, according to ground rules, there was a chill in their opening amenities as they took their adversary's measure. Then in true cattle dealer fashion he led off with melancholy remarks about the unfavorable weather conditions, the long spring drought, the dry forecast ahead, the bare country out my way, no feed, too many cattle; all bad, bad, bad. It was my first hour upon the boards in this role, but I knew vicariously all the verses to the depressing pitch. I missed all the cues by holding my tongue, which was not Hoyle: silence didn't give him a hint of how soft I was getting. He sat beside his wife on the edge of the water trough and looked at the calves bunched up in a corner eyeing him with distrust. Deeper shadows of sorrowful disapproval fell across his unmerry face. His mouth drew down and his eyes squinted. The sight of my pretty — to me they were pretty — young animals gave him the blues. Gloom, like brown smelter smoke, settled all over the hillside. I found it hard to breathe. At last, sighing, for the moment of sacrifice had been reached, he asked me what I wanted for "them little calves."

Huskily, I managed to inform him that I wanted six cents for the heifers and seven for the steers. Apparently stunned by such gall, he grunted as if in pain, shook his head, and got out a cigarette to revive himself. Now came the second big scene in his play-acting. Why, the day before he had received two hundred head of good white-faces for a nickel straight across. John Doe and Joe Doakes had bought the top yearlings from the grass country for six cents. He turned to his wife, who nodded her corroboration. I was out of line!

It was a contest in which knowledge didn't give me power. I knew they were out to wear me down and get cheap cattle. I also knew that I had no talent or taste for haggling and no skill for evading it if forced upon me. I was dumb with humiliation and disgust.

At my silence, he went into his third scene by getting up and walking about among my gentle calves, pointing out defects as if I had deliberately hidden them to hornswoggle him. One had a red neck, which, before Santa Gertrudis and Braford and such breeds were introduced into the country, used to be a mortal affliction in prospective beef animals. Each Hereford was supposed to have six to twelve inches of white on the back of his neck: two of mine had so much white they were line-backed. One was leggy, too much daylight under his belly. One was about to get pinkeye. I knew, though I couldn't dispute about it, that all this had nothing to do with the quality of meat represented by the yearlings. It was all part of the hanky-panky of bargaining.

Came the climax. He made his offer; five cents straight.

"I'm sorry," I murmured, having no stomach for dickering. "Thank you for coming."

I went to open the gate to turn my calves — which stood for the money I was desperate for — back into the little holding pasture. The offer rose to five and a-half. I went for my horse in miserable silence. As I rode out the gate he called a telephone number I could use in case I changed my mind and wanted to "do what's right."

I rode home in bitter hopelessness. The ranch world was too *western* for the likes of me. I could raise the calves and take care of them. What I couldn't do was to sell them.

The good Uncle rescued me, although he was no better a salesman than I, by giving me money and sending me to town to sit on the doorstep of the elusive old T.C., the regional buyer so deservedly cursed for false promises — yet always willing to take a chance and now and then give a leg up to the underdog. He hauled my calves to his big holding pasture — bless his heart! — and later sold them with his, for enough money to give me my original asking price and make a commission himself.

The livestock dealers steeped in sharp business practices who advise one to buy — never sell — at auctions, unquestionably know what they talk about. I can't help wondering, however, if they would have been as sanguine in the old days so well described in a letter to the *Cattle Growers' Newsletter* in which a woman wrote: "Pa argued all day with a buyer to get $7.50 apiece for his four-year-old steers."

It was the war economy that knocked the teeth out of the blood-lusting livestock dealers and traders. I had to sell cows (no rain again) in the year that Hitler marched into Poland. Old T.C. brought out a buyer to see them. When they hemmed and hawed and cried hard times, I essayed the remark that the price of cattle was bound to go up because we were going to war.

They drew back and righteously pulled their robes about them, shrinking from me in horror as if I were a witch conjuring up war, signing the death warrants of good young men that I might make a puny few dollars on my cows. "I don't want no blood money!" declared old T.C. "Hell, I sure don't," cried his associate.

How peaceful, by contrast, to individual negotiations, is

the auction sale. You may be disappointed, but no flare-up of temper need hazard a heart attack nor stir up a fist fight.

Prosperous, well-established born-to-the-range cattlemen over the years have made contacts with feeders and commission men that endure from season to season with satisfaction on both sides. The arrangement, often, is much like a partnership. They are the industry's aristocracy. Some longtime operators send their yearlings to well-fixed midwestern grain farmers every year. Some have regular stops, here in southern Arizona and in southern California, for their beef animals: from ranch to feedlot to retailers, such as supermarkets, working on a large scale. The selling and buying are all taken care of when the calves are born, or before. That is big business and it involves other people's money — banks or credit associations.

But for the independent family-size farm or ranch, and for all loners and little operators, the weekly livestock auction holds the solution to all kinds of problems. It is the handiest device that has come along since they started putting pockets in shirts.

CHAPTER 8

The Rangeland Order of the Purple Heart

A cowman, writing with waggish outdoor wit in a recent issue of *Arizona Cattlelog,* said he got hurt by "a sloppy old critter with no pride in the way she fell."

That could hardly happen here. The critters grazing my steep canyon walls have tough, surefooted sinews. They sometimes make threats — on purpose — with hoofs and horns, and are occasionally free with wallops from hard mulish heads, but none has hurt any person by accident. The only scar I bear from bovine assault is on the muscle of my left leg, where a steer gave me a kick with the fullest intention.

I had three yearlings cornered in the crowding pen, trying to load them for delivery to the Saturday auction. One was stalled in the loading chute. With a good stout stick I was punching him along when one of his buddies struck me from behind with a five-hundred-pound blow that landed a few inches below my left knee joint. A well used calf-muscle saved me from a broken leg that would surely have interrupted my cattle sale, as I was alone on the ranch at the time. But a miss is as good as a mile. I was too rushed to take much note of a non-disabling injury. I finished loading my steers, but I knew I'd been hit. A quick numbness spread through the lower half of my leg and what seemed like a foreign object attached itself where the kick had landed. When I had a chance to reach down to investigate, I found my skin stretched over an astonishing bulge as large as a grapefruit on the calf of my leg.

When the steers were in the rack, the endgate secured, and the pickup over the hazards and through the gate by the house, I splashed alcohol on the wound and went on with my cattle. It was Saturday. Civilization is so ordered that on Saturday afternoons and Sundays — usually the hours when country people come to grief — doctors hide out. A backwoodser falling sick or injured on weekends must wind up as his or her own physician. Two days later, a ruptured short saphenous vein had turned the "grapefruit" an ugly color, and a steady throb defied aspirin and hot water. The doctor frightened me with such dread words as "traumatic abscess" and "possible amputation." Dutifully I took his scoldings and shots and pills, and in five months the lump had disappeared. But it is a good thing that this did not happen to Marlene Dietrich, or a dark purple indent would have marred the biggest curve on one of those million-dollar gams.

All too often the newspapers and newscasters announce that someone on a ranch or farm has been accidentally killed or wounded. I have heard that by insurance companies only mining and space-riding are considered more hazardous. Yet rarely is farmer or rancher seriously hurt by cattle. The main cause of rural accidents is horsepower, a thing that some wag has said was far less dangerous when only horses had it. But experienced horsemen will testify that this is nothing to rely on.

It is remarkable that so little has been written about the bad public relations existing through the ages between horses and people. Every month tons of material are printed on the subject of horses — always from an idealized human point of view. But horses are dumb animals. Even Black

Beauty, who tugged at human heartstrings a century ago, told her story through a ghost writer.

Apparently the human type is susceptible to something that might be called "horse fever," analogous perhaps to gold or gambling fever. It seems to get almost everyone. School children, girls even more than boys, when they are looking for library books will say, "Do you have anything about a horse? I want to read a lot of horse books."

The trouble is that the usual horse books may be dangerous for children, spreading wrong ideas that might get them hurt. Writers of horse books seldom seem to have any knowledge of horses. They picture them as people. A ten-year-old boy catches (impossible!) a wild stallion (one of the wildest creatures on earth!) and communicates with him in the English language until he can crawl on his back and ride him home. Fantastic! But it gets printed. And sold. Perhaps publishers, like everybody else, have horse fever to the extent that they want to adopt them into the human family. The plain fact is that horses can take us or leave us, and they'd lots rather leave us. Their charm for us, nevertheless, remains universal. In every country in the world, people love to look at horses, show them, judge them, touch them, conquer them, bet on them, own them, and — most of all — ride them. There is only one Christopher Stone; he is the fellow who said, via the London *Times:* "I hate horses — they are uncomfortable in the middle and dangerous at both ends."

There are many stories told and written about horses that have displayed affection for people. Personally, I have known these equine nonconformists only by hearsay. My father has told me about a big bay "hoss" of his named Joe, who presumably returned his master's affection to the extent of saving his life a few times in the wilds of the west Texas frontier many years ago. Papa had been drawn into a six-shooter fight to help a friend. The result was disastrous and he had to leave the country at great speed. Joe was his transportation — making as much as seventy-five miles a day — and his lifeguard. Papa would come to a grassy cove near water, and under cover of darkness, unsaddle and lie down on his blankets for a few hours' rest. Joe put in the time eating and listening. At any sound that might be hostile, he would arouse his master and they'd be off and away.

In the Thirties, ranchers were not simply businessmen selling pounds of flesh. By circumstances, and sometimes by choice, they were isolated — call it independent, if you like — people who did for themselves as frontier folks have ever done. When they wanted horses, they did not order an expensive trailer and drive off to Texas or California to horse shows or sales. They raised and trained their own. To do this, they kept mares that ate the grass that might have been fattening commercial herds of beef cattle. They raised colts that often helped to keep them broke, and sometimes broke their necks.

I had a wellbred dun mare that one spring brought forth a perfect replica of herself. They were a sight to see, bounding along with their spirited airs and mother-and-daughter coats. I thought I had never possessed such an adorable creature as that filly, and made big plans and dreams for her. I called her Cha Cha, short for *muchacha,* which is Spanish for girl (long before the popular dance came into being). Her first summer I taught her the rope and how to lead, and to let me pick up her feet and pretend to pound shoes on them. When I had to leave for school she was turned out on the range, where she grew so wild and free that all her lessons had to be done over again the second summer. That's the way it went. She learned readily enough during the vacation months, and it was fun to teach her.

Came the fall, and she went back to the wild bunch. In the summer of her fourth year she taught me a lesson. I learned that whoever undertakes to gentle horses on the installment plan is sooner or later going to hit the ground harder than the tensile strength of human bones will bear.

After my downfall, I asked a professional horse breaker I had hired if he had ever acquired any broken bones.

" 'Leven," he said laconically, and catalogued them for me.

If you know anything about horses you know that they are very conservative, indeed quite set in their ways. Hard-headed reactionaries, they are opposed to change or innovation. They must invariably be saddled from the left. A rider must mount and dismount on the left side — and better not try to vary the routine. Where I made my mistake was in failing to conform to the tradition that a rider must move his pony — lead him a few steps, turn him around, or in some way untrack him — before climbing on. An omission of this routine constitutes a foul, and the horse assumes the right to penalize. In my case the penalty was four broken bones located in the left arm and the left hip.

Night after night as I lay in the hospital, tense with jangled nerves and worried mind, I relived the catastrophe. I fastened the cinch, picked up the reins, flipped the stirrup around, stepped up on my beautiful Cha Cha — and a land-mine exploded under the saddle. Doggone it, I had stayed with her all around one corral and out into the other, and the spectators thought I had the ride made. But I was getting higher and higher from the saddle and decided I'd better step off. The Uncle was stumbling around trying to catch her, crying "Stay with her, Sister! Stay with her!" I almost hit him when I made my three-point landing.

"Are you hurt?" he asked.

"No, I don't think I am," I said; then I saw my hand going off at a strange angle to my arm. Then I tried to stand up. If only I had let her stand saddled for an hour, after being ten days free in the pasture. If only I had led her out into the other corral. If only I had got my right foot into the pigeon-toed stirrup. If only I had not let the unexpected guests have the gentle horses. If only I had been born with sense!

Being thrown from a horse may have dire consequences, but it need not single one out as unqualified. Remember the then Prince of Wales — Wally's Duke of Windsor? The throne of Britain wasn't the only seat he abdicated. There was a time when he was in the newspaper regularly for being unseated by his mount. A news article about the famed Jim Shoulders, a rodeo performer who won the world's top honors for three consecutive years for riding bucking horses and Brahma bulls, listed his injuries at the age of thirty: "His collarbone has been broken three times, both arms twice, both knees twice, and an ankle once." That shows how the odds stand on horses vs. people.

The second and last — cross my fingers — disability I sustained from domesticated wild life was a broken right arm (both bones just above the wrist) suffered while tutoring a young mule. Several lessons had gone fine. This time I was showing off for a visiting cousin, a far-gone victim of horse fever. The little sorrel mule was pretty as a doll. The cousin was anxious to get his hands on her, a feeling not at all reciprocated. She let me toss the loop over her head and start walking toward her, taking up the slack. When he came up behind me she broke to run. Immediately I dropped the rope. Before I could get clear of it, the cousin grabbed it up and snubbed it around a center post. At that moment the mule whirled back, the taut rope upended me, and snap went my glass bones. To console me later the cousin said: "You were caught between a mule and a fool."

A broken arm isn't too bad. You adjust. If you are overtaken horseback in a summer rain squall, your cast will melt and you'll have to improvise some splints. In the pickup alone you will manage with your left hand, reaching across under the wheel to shift gears at a propitious moment. If the "doc" will strap an aluminum brace on your arm instead of the misery-making outmoded cast, you can poke the gears into place with it after healing begins. My two biggest problems were throwing on my saddle and fastening my bra. But with a rope thrown over a beam of the shed, I could hoist the saddle and get it on a cooperative pony. As for the garment, I simply wore the thing through my forty-two days and nights, and counted myself lucky that the weather was hot and I could shower and launder simultaneously.

Considering the inherent everlasting conflict of wills and wits between horses and mankind, we can usually feel that we are top dogs and look with a degree of tolerance on occasional rebels and rioters from the losing side. We can be generous foes because we excel in logistics and battle gear. A rebellious horse can be subdued or restrained by ropes, headstalls, cross hobbles, and torturing bridlebits; he can be punished by whip and spur; he can be sold to cruel men of evil intent. There is no law against killing him, and in the era of tranquilizers, even chemical warfare is available.

Therefore, as champions big enough to lose a battle now and then, we proffer respect and some admiration to our opponent, the horse. He is worthy of our steel. We see justification in his revolt, which springs from an instinctive urge also common to us: the eternal longing for individual freedom. We pick ourselves up, maybe with the help of bystanders, and doff our hats to him.

But what, except groans and curses, can be said for the merciless outrages committed upon our persons by the mechanical horsepower the machine age compels us to operate?

It was a cold December morning, very early, when I received my worst injury in the line of duty as engineer of a motor-driven pumping outfit.

This was at Pepper Sauce Canyon. I was going to move a bunch of cattle thirteen miles, to a barley field down on the river. My helpers were not robust which explains why I was the only one up at that hour. At any rate, it behooves the boss to be the earliest riser. Besides the good example, it gives a chance to keep an eye out for slips and mishaps. A feminine boss is doubly obligated, for she must take responsibility for breakfast and lunch. While coffee perked, biscuits baked, and the stars in their majestic courses proclaimed the dawn, I took my flashlight and stumbled down the steep trail to the pump in the canyon.

I have already made clear my opinion that a stationary gasoline engine is the biggest flop of the industrial age. In hot weather it burns itself to extinction and has to be hauled away to be reconditioned at great expense. In cold weather it won't start.

By spying on paid mechanics I had learned a number of tricks, and that frosty morning I played them all. When choking and priming and sleight-of-hand cranking had no effect, I resorted to my trump — pulling hard on the belt to the pumpjack pulley. The crude outfits by which country people raise water out of wells to put it up on hills for houses and corrals are always set low on the ground. To minister to one, you must bend into a U-turn, a position the human spine was not designed to maintain. Odds against me, I boldly set the gadgets and gave the cold sticky four-inch belt a sharp tug. Nothing happened. Angrily I straddled the belt, got a stout grip with both hands, and gave a mighty jerk with all the power of the three kinds of muscle: striped, smooth, and cardiac. Explosion took place where it ought to, the engine began firing forcefully and rhythmically as if it had meant to do so all along, and the little jack started lifting water and pushing it up the pipeline.

For me, alas, it was a Pyrrhic victory. I clung to the side of the pumphouse and got my leg over the whirring belt, then fell to the ground in agony. My right kidney — I learned much later — had been jerked loose from its moorings. Mercifully, at the time, I didn't know the extent of my injury. I thought I had pulled a muscle in my back. Ashamed of being awkward, I cussed up perseverance enough to get back up the hill and make a fair try at business as usual. Before beginning the long cold horseback ride, I went into the bathroom and strapped my back with adhesive tape and put aspirin tablets in my shirt pocket. Every outdoor person, no matter which sex, knows that the human body, driven by the human will, can and will do the impossible. My cattle got to pasture and I rode home.

Four years and five doctors later, I entered the hospital and a skillful urologist sliced a ten-inch incision in my flank, took out the roving kidney, trimmed away the adhesions of the entwined tube, and sewed it stoutly to the twelfth rib. He was proud of his work. My part was to pay for his brilliant achievement and the hospital service, and lie twenty-one days flat on my back with the foot of my bed propped up higher than the head: eighteen inches at first, then twelve, nine, six; and there never was a slower countdown. Besides being tied to the bedstake, my three-week absence nearly put me out of the cow business. Prospects for feed looked bad that June, and I needed money. I was relieved when a neighbor who knew cows well enough to start from scratch and make a fortune volunteered to gather and sell some of my old nellies. At the time, I had 120 cows, located, good-aged, named, and cherished. Before I knew what was happening, eighty of them had been gathered and sold. He calmly remarked: "Ever' damn one needed selling."

What cow doesn't, for one reason or another, need selling?

Seven years and a change of venue were behind me before my number came up again on the foul machine. Once more it was early morning. I "dawned," as getting up early is described in Spanish, to pump water before the summer sun hit the exposed pipeline. In this case, it was necessary to drive a jeep pickup nearly a mile down an improvised canyon road to get to the recalcitrant pump engine. My dictionary says *recalcitrant* in literal translation from the Latin means *kicking back*. That's my word! Two days previously, a mechanic had come out to fix the engine so it would not be so hard to start. To make it fire quickly, he retarded the spark. Ignorant of what this meant, I picked up the crank and gave it a whirl. My mistake! The doctor, later making ready to stab my right wrist with a long heavy needle, told me that when bones are shattered by a powerful blow they are in much worse shape than when broken by a fall from tripping over a rope or being thrown from a horse. I believed him. It was my right arm, the same one broken in the incident with the little mule. Needless to say, I drove the jeep back up the twisting bumpy road, since I was alone.

In this catalogue of injuries I shall pass lightly four cracked ribs — two each on different occasions. They were painful for only a couple of weeks or so, and nothing at all could be done for them. The heavy canvas straps that doctors use for binding rib cages are for men only.

Speaking of females, I have not happened to meet other women who have been seriously injured doing ranch work. But the country is full of their husbands, fathers, brothers, and sons who have made the casualty list while carrying on the daily range tasks. How does that old cowboy song about "Brown" go?

> *Before you start the cowpunching life,*
> *Go make your will and kiss your wife,*
> *And stab yourself with a butcher knife,*
> *For that's the easiest way!*

CHAPTER 9

Caring for the Green

The morning Charlie and Paul came to make the cement slab in front of my kitchen door, I was busy doctoring cows at the corral.

"We'll go ahead and make the forms," Charlie said.

When I returned, Charlie and Paul were down on their hunkers staking out the neatly arranged boards. Suddenly I gasped to see the tall green plant that had been growing to the left of the door now uprooted and leaning over against the garden fence.

"Oh! You pulled up my little tree!" I cried, and squatted down at once to begin digging like a dog at the rubble Charlie had shoveled into the tree hole.

"Why," he protested, "it's just a castor bean!"

"It came up about a year ago," I said. "Planted itself right where I wanted a green something. I kept it from freezing last winter. I put boxes around it to break the wind, and on cold nights I covered it with gunnysacks. Every morning I pour a coffeepotful of water on it."

As I spoke I filled the cleared hole with water from the hose and took up the manhandled castor bean, its straight six-foot stalk topped by a cluster of dull green leaves now doomed to wither, and replanted it in hope it might start living again. Charlie knelt and arranged the roots and patted the earth over them. He was sorry. But to him it was still only an old castor bean.

Charlie lived in town where organized society has put water and soil where Nature didn't, so that residents of the community can mask the desert in green and have their pick of vegetation. Also, he was a member of the axe-wielding sex who whacked down the virgin forests of North America without a qualm of conscience.

"I never thought you'd care about a castor bean," he apologized.

"They say they keep away flies," I said, giving my scorned plant another dash of water. I didn't hold it against Charlie. He just didn't understand the way I looked at it.

Civilization doesn't cut much ice on my little outfit. In this under-watered area of rock-bound ridges and sun-baked cliffs and gorges, any vegetable thing taking up root-rights must depend on moisture from the stingy skies of the horse latitudes. Any green thing that isn't actually obnoxious is welcome. Charlie did wonder at the trouble I took to cultivate Johnson grass and Bermuda grass, both constantly exterminated by dirt farmers. I like them because, if given water, they grow luxuriantly even in an inch or two of soil covering solid conglomerate. Another advantage is that they'll keep an old sore-eyed cow in good flesh, and when she is gone they'll come right back again.

Obviously this fondness for low-life plants marks me as a rather desperate member of the sex that clutched geranium slips and rose cuttings to its bosom through the terrors of crossing the Sea Of Darkness in windjammers; and later nourished a few sprigs of green things across the western plains in covered wagons. In this climate of seven to nine months of growing season almost any plant thrives if given water.

In my present location of many disadvantages, I do have water. (When I moved in, a neighbor said: "You have worlds of water.")

The biggest disadvantage here is that this place isn't Los Alisos, my homestead, dear to me because I built it up myself from the grass roots (there wasn't a nail or a piece of board or a scrap of any man-made material when I took it over) and made a tree-shaded little home of dramatic beauty on the rocky, flat-topped slope overlooking the sheer 60-feet high walls of the sandy canyon. It broke my heart to leave it. In a recent *Cattle-Growers' Newsletter* I read a letter written by a ranch woman who had lived in the same house for 64 years. That's the kind of history I wish I could have had.

The Old Vaquero called the Pepper Sauce Place *Rancho Sal si Puedes* (Get-Out-If-You-Can Ranch) because the road hazard was so formidable. (It still is. Although it became a part of an affluent ranch to the west and the owners bulldozed two roads into the rough canyon and spent thousands of dollars remodeling and decorating the main cabin and the guest house, no one has lived there since I left. It is too inaccessible. The bulldozed roads wash out as fast as they are made; and nobody but me ever attempted to navigate the deep sand in the canyon.)

I stayed on with the help of my "three old men," my good sister Ruby after she was widowed, an occasional hired hand, and some of my pupils who came to visit as well as labor.

I stayed on even after that sad day for many cows on the range when Progress took over the San Pedro River Valley. A big mining company, backed by a big government loan, began pouring millions of dollars into the cholla flats and rocky ridges and greasewood mesas of our back country as well as into the barley and alfalfa fields and mesquite *montes* (thickets) of the bottomland. Giant operations began groping for ore in a copper-bearing mass two thousand feet underground of a vastness guaranteed to last for fifty years. Housing projects sprang up. Artesian wells were drilled. Finally, a brand-new twenty-million dollar town, complete with electricity, plumbing, and landscaping, came into being in the midst of my most northern cholla sections. That was how Progress got me. I resisted. I said *no* for three years to the sharp dealers sent out to handle me. But in a contest between a foolish woman, up to her neck in poverty, and a multi-million-dollar corporation, is there any doubt who wins? They were patient. They investigated me. One day a high-priced lawyer who had kissed the blarney stone brought me over to see this place which the company had bought three years previously and let the grass grow up. It looked too rough. I couldn't see my old cows climbing up and down the funnel-like sides of this wide, far-off canyon. Then he took me down to the spring. It is a wonderful spring, the best, according to oldtimers, in all these mountains. I sat there looking at the clear stream which rippled along and jumped over the wall of the concrete cistern that spans the creek and found it hard to tear myself away. I was bewitched. My well at home, which we had deepened twice over the years and dug a tunnel out under the creekbed for storage, had only six inches of water in it. And the Uncle and I were suckers for trees — he for fruit trees and I for shade trees. Under the spell of the lovely water I signed a scrap of paper that didn't seem to have much importance but turned out to be as binding as if it bore the great seal of the nation. No complaints. I did not get a good price, but I got a fair price. And the magic spring is mine.

The company kindly helped transplant my outfit root and branch, lock, stock, and barrel, to my present smaller holdings in the rugged Galiuro Mountains, forty miles across the Valley from my homestead. When the sorrowful move was made I clung with maternal tenacity to my cows.

And my horses. And my dogs. And my three old men. The year before, I had bought a new pickup. Ruby had the old one. I bought a new Jeep pickup which was driven by a hired cowboy. These three little trucks crawled like ants across the Valley for five months. We carted over first the cows with baby calves. Then the heavy cows soon to calve. The rest of the cattle were brought over in a three-day drive with arrangements made to corral them at night at ranches along the river. We tore down corrals, and rebuilt them over here. We dug out windows and doors because the agent who was in charge of dealing with me said that the company was interested only in the land. "You can take the house if you want to," he said. "But you have a big old stone house over there you can fix up and take in boarders if you want to."

It isn't a stone house. It has a stone foundation to a height, on two sides, of about four feet. The adobes it is made of had been plastered to look like cement. The builder, who at the time was superintendent of the mine then flourishing two miles up the canyon, had in mind a Mexican ranchhouse. In a great square he built a series of box-like rooms enclosing a cement-floored patio which was almost entirely roofed over and was broken into by a twelve-by-thirty-two foot living room. He suffered from hayfever, so he left only a small square of dirt in the patio and there planted an arbor vitae. Mary Ann, his daughter, told me that when they lived here it was a pretty, round green ornamental plant barely reaching to the roof. When the owner died and the mine closed down, the family scattered. A neighboring rancher bought the land and water (everything was cheap in those days) and the house was left to vandals. For ten years the abandoned old house was a target for men and boys with destruction as their aim. They carried off everything that wasn't nailed down: cupboards, doors, windowscreens; they couldn't dislodge the steel-casement windows so they shot out the glass panes.

The first view I had of the devastated place repelled me. It looked like the ruins of an old fort left to the ravages of time. It was sun-beaten, stark, bare as the ridge of Gila conglomerate on which it stood — a kind of natural concrete that has survived millions of years of erosion without being reduced to fertile soil. Chollas, the fish-hook bristling cactus that seems to jump at you, grew close around it.

It was when I walked to the front door of the patio (there were only two entrances to the building — front and back through the patio) that I felt a pang of sympathy. There was that arbor vitae, now turned into a half-grown tree with many dead limbs protruding on all sides, still struggling to live, starving for water. The first thing I did when I took possession was to haul a barrel of water to pour on it.

We (the Uncle, the Old Vaquero, the Star Boarder, Ruby, and I) chased the pack rats out of the house, chased the wild pigs from under the neglected hardwood floors, killed the wasps in the eaves, and the snakes lurking under old piles of rotting lumber and other trash. We fenced two acres for a yard and cleared away the offending cactus.

The company installed a gasoline-powered pump and laid 4,000 feet of two-inch pipeline up to the house, 286 feet higher than the spring. We laid another 300 feet of line up to a big cement tank to store water for the house and the corrals. Dave's father, a miner, came over and blasted holes for the thirteen fruit trees we brought here from the homestead; and Dave and I went to the river and dug up a young cottonwood and a willow, both, alas, gluttons for water.

We had doors and windows put in; Ruby cleaned and polished the floors; we brought over our household things

— the three little pickups crawling back and forth like ants over the old abandoned road. We at last got the county road crew to scrape it, a job they hadn't had to bother with for years. And in five months we were moved in and had started another ranch. This ranch. The GF Bar as of today.

It is based on the wonder spring that bubbles up in good quantities out of a fault in the bedrock down in the creek channel a mile below the house, and sparkles off in a bright stream through a narrow box canyon over almost solid stone for several hundred yards before finding its way back into the earth cracks. This spring must have been treasured by animals and human beings for thousands of years. It is, however, located in a soilless place where it can nurture only a few brave willows, a tenacious hackberry, and a stunted sycamore. No cowman in the world would build his house so far uphill above his water source. Only a mining man, expecting to make a million dollars almost any day, will attempt such an expensive undertaking. The excuse I have for the folly of carrying on the operation of putting water uphill such a distance is that I like cows and love greenery and am permanently under the spell of that wonderful gushing spring.

The old house's nudity was intolerable. I couldn't wait to clothe it with flowers and vines and trees. Trees first of all. The young fruit trees we transplanted, except the few that died, began to thrive in their new quarters and I could see their pretty green leaves when I got near enough. But I wanted tall green screening trees that could be seen from the hilltop a mile away. I longed for swaying boughs that could be bird shelters and catch the song of the night winds as those at the homestead had done for many years. That's why Dave and I went to the river for the cottonwood and willow. They grew obligingly and were no burden while they were young. If the pump broke down there was still plenty of water down at the spring and I could carry it to them by means of a barrel and a bucket. In my nostalgia I failed to realize that trees and water have some kind of ratio that goes into high mathematics. One that in the beginning got along fine on five gallons of water a day now sops up fifty gallons and reaches for more.

When you move into an unimproved place, friends and neighbors come bearing gifts of slips and cuttings, most of which — because your yard is bare and theirs is over-supplied — are spreaders: mint, myrtle, mile-a-minute vine, and honeysuckle. You give them water, and they grow and spread and want more water and grow more and want more until you wake up to the fact that you are caught in a cycle that consumes your time and money. But if you have my weakness for growing things you won't regret it.

From the rim of the canyon, where the road gives the first glimpse into its depths, this place strikes the beholder as an oasis in the depressingly dry environs. Magnetically, it catches the eye of the driver making slow progress in second gear down the long mile to the gate. If my visitors are women or greenhorns, they exclaim with pleasure at the jungle of green leaves and colorful flowers. If by chance a cowman is in the group, he says nothing, takes it all in, gives me some speculative looks, and perhaps finds an opportunity to offer to buy me out at a ridiculous figure. He has reason to judge me a fool. I confess that my determination to live in a green spot, if it kills me, is pure folly a man would not indulge in. Actually it rates me as being at the bottom of the class in cowmanship. Cattle range wouldn't be cattle range if it were well-watered, or even moderately damp. In our long growing season it would be, if not a jungle, at least a forest. And plants such as mine (whose sole use is spiritual) are hard-drinking organisms.

It is not that their *"aqua-holism"* deprives any beast of a mouthful of water. In this limited space it would not be possible to run enough cows to drink all the water in the creek. But in a sense my cattle do suffer, for the cost of running a gasoline pump several hours a day would buy considerable hay. And the daily hours spent dragging four hoses from clump to clump of ever-thirsting roots could be profitably spent in riding out to see about the dogies. Thus, as in all tippling, the sin is manifest.

The morning glories are the worst topers. Leaves, stems, and blossoms, they are ninety-five per cent water. Years ago I put ten cents worth of seeds of the big blue variety into the ground to tone the bareness of my sahuaro-rib fence. I have never planted any since. But here they are, in different colors now, all over the place. It is culpable to water them, for two days later they'll need twice as much because they will have doubled in size. Short-budgeted, pressed for time, I resolve to pull them up and throw them away. Then comes daylight, I step out of my door, and there they stand arrayed in morning glory, greeting me in a crescendo of joy. I turn on the hoses and go down to fight the pump into action.

Cattle kings of the Old West generated some unfavorable publicity in their ruthless battle against the dry farmers and other dirt-poor nesters who crept into their public domain holdings and tried to grow plants domestically. A few generations later, agricultural experts conceded that fundamentally the ranchers were right. They had Nature on their side. The only way to make two blades of grass grow where one grew before, is to give the roots twice as much water as is available. Today's cowmen, born to the business (and carrying on with, as often as not, ever less success), have a similar aversion to landscaping. They know it takes precious water and essential time. In the outlying places of the semi-arid Southwest, when you drive up to a country house that is set among stately trees and spacious lawns, you have not come to a working ranch, but to the isolated estate of eastern people who have made money enough in other climates to afford costly irrigation under clear skies and a warm sun.

A few years ago, a ranch not far from my homestead was bought by a gentleman who had a seat on the stock exchange on Wall Street. He paid a king's ransom, the neighbors said, for the water from a mine tunnel in the mountains four and a half miles above his house — and he put in a pipeline to bring it down. They figured it would take a whale of a lot of cows a long time to have calves enough to pay that out. But when they heard the next plan they stopped figuring and stood in jaw-dropping amazement. The man's wife proposed to grow roses the entire length of the pipeline. Quite a dream; over four miles of roses winding down the barren rocky foothills. A few years later, when the dreamers were rudely awakened to facts, they returned to the Land of Money and Rain, where roses are everywhere. And a law suit tied up the pipeline.

It cannot be denied that, as a rule, men are the romantic adventurers and women the practical beings. Nevertheless, through the makeup of a woman runs a soft streak that makes her a sucker for green leaves and bright posies. She is wooed with flowers; carries them at her wedding; displays them on her tables; nurtures them in her garden. And surely it was a woman who first placed the assuaging beauty of flowers on the grave.

This yearning is in addition to the fact that women were probably the world's first farmers — gathering fruits and seeds for food, planting and tending the best specimens.

Among many primitive people women are still the farmers. This love of green things growing is not for bread alone, but seems to arise from an instinct of the female to want to force Nature to function over and above the survival line. In the poorest shacks — even in migrant workers' hovels — that house women, one will find something growing, if only in old lard pails and coffee cans.

When we take off the rose-colored glasses, it is plain to see that Nature is ever of two minds: to create and to destroy. The number and variety of plants in Southern Arizona (which an esteemed botanist has called an "arboreal desert") are something to marvel at. How can so much grow during the months that the brassy skies produce so little measurable moisture?

On a hot July day a dozen weeks or so after the last rain, the trees, bushes, and root-grass appear as brittle and lifeless as skeletons, and gray with dust. Comes a summer shower, and in a few days the countryside sparkles with green. It is a miracle hard to credit.

When I first walked over the six-hundred-forty acres of my homestead, I was delighted to count eleven varieties of trees growing on it: mesquites, palo verdes, catclaws, hackberries, dwarf oaks, stunted cedars (junipers), desert willows, black walnuts, two small slender ash trees, and, down by the well, a big sycamore and a giant cottonwood with a girth of seventeen feet.

Of all the native trees in the Southwest, I dare say the mesquite has been of greatest value to man and livestock. It is sad to know that of late years Progress has condemned this hardy perennial to destruction by bulldozers and death-dealing chemicals — not only where it thrives along rivers where the bottomland is to be cleared for farming, but also far out on dry prairies and hillsides where it is often the only upstanding vegetation that will grow.

I love the mesquite for its beauty and usefulness. Given half a chance, its trunks and branches arrange themselves with a symmetry pleasing to the most exacting eye. Its leaves are intricately graceful. In springtime, the loveliest color in rangeland is that of its tender new green. Its yellow blossoms, protected by businesslike thorns, are fragrant feasts for bees and butterflies and other insect life. Its roots will reach astonishing depths to pick up precious water, or on rock-based land, run laterally for twenty to forty or more feet to gather moisture and store it up against a rainless day.

Mesquite trunks and branches make good fence posts and good firewood. They were used as beams by the cliff-dwellers, and some still exist to be studied by anthropologists and archeologists. The early padres and their native converts used mesquite wood in their missions: some of the carved doors and lintels at Tucson's San Xavier Mission have endured for close to two centuries. Mesquite gum was used by Indians to make dye and cement for their pottery. The bark has been used for medicine. As for its beans, dried, it would be hard to name anything growing in cattle country more nourishing to animals. The U. S. Cavalry bought them by the pound for their horses. The Indians that knew of them, ate them. Even dogs eat them.

It seems wicked to eradicate this wonderful plant that through ages inhospitable with so many great droughts has provided man with beauty, comfort, shelter, wood for his fires and his buildings, food for himself and his beasts. I am grateful for the fecund mesquites that grow along the creek here, giving shade and browse to my cattle in the seasons of heat and dryness.

As for my cultivated plants, a true gardener would never accept me into his guild. My flowers are not grown; they grow — volunteer and helter-skelter. The rains bring them up, then carelessly cease their life-giving function, and the young plants that survive do so at my mercy and expense. The trouble and cost of watering them can be discounted, for they come with built-in rewards. Beyond my doorstep are zinnias, shoulder-high, splashing pink and red and yellow under a blue sky, enticing the silent, tireless, yellow butterflies. Four-o-clocks, vigorous and profuse, grow to a height of seven feet and spread greedily over the enclosure, so that I have to paw my way through them to move the hose. Roses and honeysuckle vie for a place atop the fence — the rose winning by a triumphant pink and yellow bud. And everywhere there are morning glories, blue-violet, with red-violet veins and fluffy white centers and a look of deep-piled velvet. At night the birds flutter in the branches of the trees, and crickets stir up a symphony. The shadowy lushness of leafy branches and the distillation of plant perfumes give one a sense of being transported to another land.

There is no day in the year that I cannot find a bloom of some kind in my yard. In the fall there are yellow and orchid chrysanthemums. In December and January there are late roses and early violets. The fruit trees come out in February and March (and often get nipped by frost). Then come the irises and other bulbs. And summer rushes in again with a riot of everything, frothed up by a new crop of volunteer morning glories. The truth is that I ought to have to pay an excise tax on my garden spot, for it is a luxury in a definite dictionary sense: "something which conduces to enjoyment over and above the necessaries of life; hence something which is desirable but not indispensable."

CHAPTER 10

They'll Never Be Missed

Civilization, with all its achievements, ought to provide some better excuse than a hunting season to get townfolk out in the open — if for no other reason than their inability to distinguish between the wilderness (which presumably belongs to everybody) and somebody's back yard.

American heritage includes the tenet of English common law that everyman's house is his castle, where he can be private and secure. He can, that is, if his house is in a well-policed city or town. A rural house is a magnet, drawing in a great many more than invited guests and friends. Some of the urbanized public — cooped-up during the week in office, factory, shop, limited home quarters, the maze of streets and utility alleys — take to the open country when they get a chance and go overboard about what they think is primitive adventure.

A stranger rouses you out at dawn, and when you call off the dogs he asks permission to go through your yard fence and down the canyon by your private road (such as it is) to your spring to try to surprise a deer that innocently may be getting a drink before the day's run for its life. Some do not even ask for permission.

Another stranger, searching the premises until he finds you down at the corral milking your cow, asks where he can find a wild pig to shoot. He has come all the way from California to get his javelina (peccary). This, he expects, will touch your cold heart, and you'll be happy to stop your chores and direct him to a victim.

Still another brings his wife and child down to the house at your siesta hour because he has read your "No Hunting" sign, and wants special dispensation for Johnny, who is already eleven years old and has never killed a deer, so this year he must get one. In deference to Johnny, who looks more embarrassed than bloodthirsty, you smile when you search for polite words that mean no.

Not all uninvited visitors come to kill. A retired man and his wife, winter visitors with time on their hands and the big outdoors to put to some purpose, are driving around for pastime. They see your house and turn in at the forks of the road to have a look at what, to them, seems to be a real ranch far out in the wilds. (Ten miles!) They want to find out who lives on it and how prosperous it is; above all, how many cattle it will run. No escape. There it is — the intrusive disconcerting point-blank question: *How many cattle do you have?* (One way of asking how much money you have.) A dude-wrangler, with more knowledge of humans than bovines, taught me the answer to that presumptuous question: "Two Jersey cows and a borrowed bull." But, to innocent greenhorns?

For us who live in remote places, there will always be unknown and uninvited callers: the numberless multitudes who, having nothing better to do, see a road and follow it; see a house and — especially if it has a tree growing out of the middle of it — stop because — well, because it is there.

A well-to-do well-dressed and, if it can be said, well-automobiled couple who live in a new town nearby, drove up the canyon one Sunday afternoon and stopped for a surprise call. I was in dirty Levi's and a beat-up hat, breathless from a battle with the pump engine, which gets no

Sundays off. They sat in the patio and drank lemonade and looked at the clutter and the junky furniture, found they were slumming, and gently departed.

How about turning the tables? If on a summer day I am driving through their landscaped town and see their beautiful lawn, bright flowers, and attractive residence, suppose I park my dirty old pickup against their curb and walk up the curving path to ring their doorbell and say I'd like to look *their* place over!

In my situation, remote as it is from modern standards of living, whenever the "Public" puts on a red hunting hat and arms himself to invade the domain of my unsuspecting range cows in the name of sport, I am inclined to believe that a first-class damning is what he needs. To one out in the sticks he appears as a dangerous vandal with blood in his eye and pillage in his wake.

The damage he does in rural areas throughout the West is not the less for being in many cases unintentional. In an issue of *Cattle Growers' Newsletter* a rancher wrote that a part of his range had dried up, so he opened a gate to let the seventy head of cattle in that pasture go to water in the next one. Along came a "crazy hunter" and closed the gate. (No doubt he was thinking of all the publicity about hunters leaving gates open.) Before the rancher discovered this mistake, all except ten hardy cows had died of thirst.

My losses from weapon-carrying invaders seem small by this scale, but they prorate, and they have seldom been unintentional. Riding up the canyon less than a mile from the house, I found a dead cow, still warm, lying close to the road. Evidence showed that she had been eating on a bush a few yards up the slope when hit over the left eye by a bullet fired, probably, from a moving vehicle, and had plunged headlong through brush and cactus to die near the killer's path. She was a good young cow I called Despiada (Tenderfoot) and was soon to calve. Farther up the road lay a snake with the head shot off. This Sport was a crack shot, an accomplishment not common among amateur hunters.

I once stood beside my excited horse and heard a hunter firing across the great canyon, perhaps, as the crow flies, about a mile away — too far, at least, through impassable country, for me to do anything about it — and counted sixteen shots, bang-bang-bang, in rapid-fire succession; a pause; then four more shots dwindling in sound as the rifleman moved over the ridge. What kind of gunner was it that couldn't hit a cornered deer — these canyons and gullies are nothing but corners — with all those chances?

The neighbors were gathering cattle, but they had trouble on the roundup because of the volleys and charges of deer-missing hunters. Trying to drive down one canyon toward their home pasture, they encountered thirty-seven hunters in less than three miles; each encounter made a scatterment of Brahmas. When Joyce—the owner—went into the village and called the Game and Fish Commission, they told her that because of a shortage of tax money the state could not afford to hire wardens for this area.

When I hear shots after dark, sometimes late at night (flashlight or spotlight hunters?) I go out and blow the horn on the pickup, longing to blow up the hoodlum night-sports, for whoever they are, they're not serious hunters. No true hunters are that meat-hungry any more.

Years ago, when ranchers were country-dwellers, I had some neighbors who were real frontier hunters. They used guns to get something to eat; if they got nothing, they went without meat with their beans and biscuits. The master hunter of the clan was a lean, lanky, ruddy-faced blond who was the freest human being I ever met. He wanted very little from the world, so he gave it no hostages and few compromises. He lived in a shack apart from his brother, who was tied down by a family so that he had to take $30-a-month jobs and sometimes ask for flour from the Relief. The Hunter, being a bachelor and capable of supplying most of his wants except tobacco and matches, had avoided such traps and chains. I'm sure he never saw Ambrose Bierce's *The Devil's Dictionary,* but his way of life proved him a believer in its definition of Labor: "one of the processes by which *A* acquires property for *B.*" Free of the desire for things most people feel are necessities, he would not take a permanent job, and very few temporary ones. If you were in a fix because your well had to be deepened, or the flood had torn out your pipeline, he would obligingly help you a few days. Okay whatever you paid him.

Ordinarily the Hunter's time was spent in the open. He knew how many quail were in the vicinity, and where they nested. He knew where the deer and wild pigs were, and just how to bring in their flesh with the least effort and ammunition. He wasn't shooting for fun; so he didn't bother about the red tape of licenses. Of course, when wild animals were scarce he killed a beef — most likely one of mine since they were handiest. I vaguely knew this, but I forgave him because he was so darn good at it that it was months before the animal was missed, if ever: there was no chance of coming upon worrisome evidence. Also, he did it purely and simply to have meat for his brother's children as well as for himself. You can understand the call of need. It is the neighbors who are clumsy and careless and money-greedy — saving their own to sell — who get your dander up when they eat your cattle.

Hunters like these old boys — the brother was no slouch — are seldom pests. In their way they are experts, and deserve a certain acclaim. They belong to a time that has passed. Both men are dead now. But their skill with guns has been passed on. The brother's wife, still my friend, is the feminine equivalent of a good hunter. She came this way with two young sons the first day of last hunting season, from their place down on the river. I don't know how early they went up the canyon, but at ten that morning they had their deer and were headed home when I met them. With them it was not sport, but a job to be done.

It is on account of the unqualified amateurs that ranchers post their ranges and lock their gates. Sports demand skill in handling paraphernalia; but you need not know much about a gun to be allowed to go out and kill. Society has not yet devised sufficient target-shooting tests and other qualifications for the applicants who want permission to make themselves at home all over the countryside while applying themselves to the killing of defenseless creatures. So far, all you need in order to enjoy the brutal pleasure of seeing a living thing fall when you pull the trigger are a firearm, ammunition, and the license fee.

Death is acceptable in this pain-racked universe, and I can also accept wisecracks or sanguine wit such as "kicked the bucket," and "turned up his toes" that are sometimes used to describe the final exit of one's fellow man. But nothing humorous can be thought or said about the dumb slow agonies of suffering creatures casually wounded and left to die by inches.

There is a place high up on a steep ridge, in plain sight of the house, that I have tried never to pass since I saw there the remains of a buck that had been shot but not killed and had tried unsuccessfully to jump the barbed-wire fence. Coming upon the bodies of what once were respectable, even beautiful, animals that had been eaten alive by screwworms after being wounded brings to mind the observation of the dejected old rabbit: *"People are no damn good."*

Over in what would be a meadow if chollas were tall grass instead of cactus, not half a mile from the house, lived a mother doe and her two pretty fawns. When I rode there I waited on my ridge until she and her young ones had clambered gracefully over the opposite one. Sometimes they stopped and gazed at me as I moved slowly in and out of the brush and cactus. I liked to see how close I could get. Now I wish that every time I saw them I had yelled and whooped and tried to chase them, in order to give them a deadly fear of people. On Saturday before the season closed on Sunday, I went to hunt a steer yearling and rode up on the dead body of one of my little fawns. It had been shot in the breast, but not by accident. Its throat had been cut — proof that it had been killed just for the hell of it.

It is not always the dumb, under-gifted delinquents who make the inhumane errors. One Sunday, during deer season, I started out from the homestead to ride over to the Big Tank. To sustain myself during the sixteen-mile round trip I put an orange in my chaps pocket. Over the high ridge from the house, miles from any road, I came upon an armed and red-hatted Sport, all tuckered-out. He was one of a group of college boys who had left their car up on the mountain highway several miles away, and he now found himself alone and lost in this deep narrow canyon. I gave him directions to the highway and, since he was thirsty, my orange. I'd gone barely a quarter of a mile around a couple of bends when I heard him rattle off a fusillade of rifle shots. Surely, if there had been a deer near we would have alerted it! I was right to feel apprehensive. A few days later the milk cow's yearling, a brindled steer that I had passed grazing on the hillside a little way above where I met the college boy, showed up at the corral with worms on both sides of his neck. The bullet had passed through the flesh without touching bone or artery.

And I had given the scoundrel my orange!

A heifer we found shot through the neck down at the windmill had died immediately. Apparently she had been lying in the shade of a thick bush several yards from the water, and never knew what hit her. There was no evidence of a struggle. Probably she made no attempt to get up.

From the evidence, we deduced that a group of hunters had stopped to get water, and had looked around long enough to pick up a good wrench and a gallon of engine oil. Then, finding themselves still in possession of the lonely station, perhaps without bovicidal intent but merely to test their prized guns, they had shot a few rounds of cartridges. My heifer happened to stop one. They may never have known that she was there.

If I had a voice in making regulations, I would confine roving gunmen to areas not populated by country folks and their livestock. And I would confine the ownership of guns to those able to prove their responsibility and, above all, their skill.

CHAPTER 11

Under the Weather

A poet (Paul Hamilton Hayne, in "A Storm in the Distance,") wrote these lyrical lines:

> *The leveled lances of the rain*
> *At earth's half-shielded breast*
> *take glittering aim.*

I saw a rain like that one time. It was lovely. It was twice lovely, because it was mine, the whole wonder and sweep of it falling almost exclusively on our little place, and nobody was out in it but me.

At this rain view of a lifetime, I had a loge seat in a great balcony overlooking the countryside for miles around. I had seen the skyful of clouds gather into one dark mass heading directly up our canyon. And although you can never be sure until it starts pouring down, it appeared that we were to be blessed with a widely-scattered shower, the only summer kind we get in the semi-arid Southwest. I hurried my horse in an effort to get home, batten down the hatches, and give welcome to the rain. It outraced us. At the crest of the high ridge on the south side of the canyon, (the vantage viewpoint of our whole ranch on Pepper Sauce), I stopped my excited pony, who wanted to get to shelter before the rain began pounding his head, and watched the rushing storm — if a passing shower can be so designated.

Ahead of the dark blue cloud, a strong swift wind came roaring like a motorcycle vanguard crying: "Make way! Make way for Rain!" My horse refused to face it, so I grabbed my hat and half-turned in the saddle to watch the sublime display of the rain god putting on his first act of the season. Just as the curtains tore apart for the downpour, the sun broke through a rift in the western clouds to turn the dashing raindrops to silver, filling the wide, deep valley before me with millions of glittering lances, each separate and distinct, each, memory insists, at least a thousand feet long and coming in at a slant. I gloried in the sight. All rains in this country are wonderful, but this one took the prize.

My protesting pony tossed his head and stamped his feet when the heavy raindrops rushed up the hill to strike us, and I loosened reins to let him have his way down the steep trail. We rushed through the wind and the rain and the fresh aroma of damp earth, and the splashing drops pelted the ground and bounced up again in fine spray. In quick glances I saw far below me the tossing branches of the trees around the red-roofed cabin, and the tall, swaying stalks of the green cornpatch in the backyard. By the time we reached home, the shower had passed on, to lose itself in the clouds and mists of the high mountains up the creek. Behind, it left a world refreshed and sparkling clean. All the little gullies ran red with muddy water that broke into high waves over the rocks, and a dark flood roared between the canyon's steep banks and high ridges for perhaps an hour.

This memorable shower came before a drought cycle set in and the world of our great (mostly underground) river dried up. That summer the canyon ran moderately — not disastrously — every Friday for five weeks. There was plenty of water in the well down in the creek bed. All the

hills were green with root grass. All the cholla flats were green with six-weeks grass. And the cattle were fat and contented — in spite of the tormenting hordes of flies hatched out by the dampness. That was a good year.

Nobody yet knows what vast atmospheric connivances and disturbances bring good rainy seasons to western plains, mountains, and deserts. Nobody knows how or why a drought begins, or what makes it hang on to become a disaster. The fact is that we still know very little about weather, particularly the sources of life-giving rain. In geography classes, we point out the pictures in the texts and go to the board to draw crude outlines of the water-cycle: the arrows showing evaporation up to the cold layer of air where the moisture gathers and condenses into nimbus clouds which, as more arrows show, return to earth as precipitation. The pupils listen, fascinated. They know well the value of adequate rainfall. They take in the logical words and the simplifying pictures. Then a bright one's mind starts to work.

"But why, Teacher, why does it quit? Why doesn't the water-cycle go on working so that we get rain every summer when we need it?"

Well, I tell them the bit about the horse latitudes, and the gimmick about the mountains knocking down the clouds before they get over the hump to us, as they sometimes do, and — oh, well, never mind. Learn the states and capitals.

It is a pity we know so little about weather. We know what weather does, and how to use it when it is behaving right, but we do not know what it is. We know we have good seasons, and, more often, bad seasons; but what causes them is still a mystery. Now and then we get hints such as the ill winds that ravage the populace and property of the southeastern American coasts as hurricanes, blowing us good, by whirling moisture into the dry Southwest on the outer fringes of their fury. But generally, we know so little about air masses we do not even know for sure why they move from west to east.

Right after World War II, in which weather study and weather forecasting played so vital a part, both science and industry (agricultural especially) were vividly awakened to the latest development in meteorology, and in experiments being carried on not only to forecast weather accurately, but to control weather — how about that! Ranchers, talking together or writing to their newsletters and other publications, were excitedly interested. What if scientific (or artificial) rain-making should really come to pass? What? Elysian fields right here on our bare rockpiles? At least there might be a little something going on that it would pay to know about. The less conservative, nothing-ventured-nothing-gained ranchers in our dried-up rangeland joined forces, each according to his means, and gambled on the idea of cloud-seeding, sometimes called cloud-milking. I was the only non-masculine member in the deal, and not one of the most hopeful, and probably not one of the most welcome. But was there a choice? Right in the middle of the most progressively daring group, I couldn't let them say the woman had chickened. I eked out my ante. And lost. I didn't get a drop in the new dirt reservoir the federal government so generously scraped out on the waterless half of my state-leased land.

There were clouds. Everybody said: "I never saw so many clouds and so little rain." No doubt the young civilian pilot hired by the association buzzed them according to plan. He kept records and charts of his cloud-spraying activities. And I heard one man (whose ranch was across the mountains) say that he saw the plane fly into a big white cloud which immediately darkened and settled down to rain.

The experiment, however, could not be called a success. For the next few years, there were newspaper reports of cloud-seeding over many parts of the West. But apparently it was too soon. More research was needed.

Rain is the difference between having a ranch and going broke, as plenty of experienced men who were raising cattle in the twenties can tell you. In those days, when it quit raining and prices fell to nothing, many a good cowman had to give up and get a job as dude-wrangler or peace officer. A grand old fellow known to all in this area, a legend in his own lifetime for his champion roping skills and his long service as sheriff of a neighboring county, told me of having to sell out his ranch. Too many dry years sent the prices down to nothing. He borrowed money and fed what he could. Still it didn't rain. He borrowed more money and sent his cows off to distant pastures. But nothing paid off. It meant ever more borrowing as the long drought held. Finally, creditors found a buyer and sold him out for just enough to pay up. "I woke up one morning," he said, "broke — without a cow to my name — but happy. I didn't owe airy son-of-a-bitch a dime in the world."

Times have changed. Things do get better here on earth in spite of communism, imperialism, pro-and-anti-socialism, unionism, corporationism, conservatism, automationism, ignorantism, and plain old stubbornism. As proof, consider the disaster of drought and how its death-dealing sieges can be counterattacked in the present day. It is true that ranchers, living on hope, take chances when they should know better. Before they take over a range, they can ride across it and see signs that little rain falls there. The flora tells the story. Cactus and stunted bushes shield the bareness in areas of meager rainfall. But grass, very good grass, grows under and around these hard-bitten plants when it happens to rain. When nothing has eaten this grass and Indian wheat and filaree for two or three years, a covering mat of dried sprigs looks tempting enough to the cowman (or fool woman) to take a chance on. What if it is a dry season? "It will rain again. It always has."

When it doesn't, and the feed is short, he sells some of his herd if it has rained enough in other parts to keep up the price for cattle. When it still doesn't rain, and a dry winter comes after a dry fall after a dry summer after a dry spring — and perhaps even after a dry preceding winter — all is not lost. He can feed. And keep on waiting.

Dry years used to mean certain death. Some forty years ago the Uncle had a little bunch of cows on his river place. During a serious drought, eighty-two of them starved to death. On the big ranch west of my homestead, old-timers have told me, cattle died that year in such numbers you could walk all around a waterhole on their dead bodies without touching the ground.

Now, thanks to the availability of cottonseed meal (Arizona has many thousands of acres of irrigated cotton fields), and to the success of experiments on new mixtures for feed, the vagaries of the weather are somewhat less critical. With "Booster mix," also known as "cake," "range booster pellets," and "booster cubes," large numbers of cattle can get enough protein and minerals to sustain them in tough times, with what browse and cactus they can get for roughage. The "booster" feeds will not fatten, but will keep the cows in good enough shape to live and bring forth calves.

I have never had a cow die of hunger, but I have seen others' cows that did. Some self-made cowmen do not believe in interfering with nature when it costs money. They take their losses, and make them up in other ways. They do not have my chicken heart. When I see a cow starving I suffer with her. Before the salt-meal mix was concocted and sold in feed stores, I had some cows one dry summer that hung around before my eyes threatening to die if I didn't feed them. I fed them. I sold my diamond rings and bought cottonseed cake and hulls, which were very expensive. Of course it didn't take long to come to the end of my diamonds, but Old Lize and Old Dulce and their pals held on until it rained.

It is possible now to prepare for dry times, because weather forecasts (compliments of our federal government and accurate perhaps eight times out of ten) are obtainable by all. Not too long ago, long-range forecasts could be had only by those with cash to pay certain meteorologists who ran their own private services. And not too long ago, radio stations threatened to quit broadcasting weather reports unless enough listeners wrote in to make them feel it worthwhile. A few times I bought a dozen postal cards and forged the names of friends and neighbors, hoping to keep the good words on the air.

Living on a ranch, if you miss the weather report your day is ruined. Yet, even as you listen — "mostly clear today and tomorrow with little change in temperature" — you don't take the prediction at face value. You hope it's wrong. Sometimes it is. The wind can change. The clouds come up fast. And somewhere it may shower. Seldom where you want it, of course. Your outfit is too small a target for Old Jupiter Pluvius, who is blind as a bat, anyway. For the first week or two of the season of hope (beginning about San Juan's Day, June 24) you look up as you go about your tasks and see a shower curtain trailing somewhere along the slopes of the wide Valley or along the mountain rims. Somebody is getting it; some poor old cows will be benefited. Maybe tomorrow, maybe someday, it will be your turn.

Weeks go by. You see the clouds come up every day, gather, and toss off a shower up the river or down the river. Your place is still dry as a powder house. The cows fall off. The ground parches. The stunted growth shrinks to gray, bone-dry sprigs. Nothing to do but wait and hope, and get a "crick" in your neck from watching the fruitless skies.

Then it rains right up to your pasture fence and quits at the gate. That's too much! There's no sense in personal malice from the rain gods. "Not fair!" you cry, knowing how silly you are, for the only gleam of justice in the whole universe is that which feebly glows in the mind of man. Nevertheless, the injustice stabs like a knife. You get in the pickup and leave the place, half-superstitiously hoping that if you aren't there to watch, a little puckish cloud may dash in and give you a surprise break. Returning, you pass through two or three cool refreshing showers and try not to get your hopes up. *It's bound to be dry at home.* You're right. And it's hard to take.

One wretched summer day I was down at the Windmill tending the hungry cattle. I watered the little patch of Johnson grass in the shanty yard while the cows ate their daily ration of range booster, filled up on water and fresh air, and started to lie down in the shade to rest until the shank of the evening. Then I saddled my pony and undertook, with a long, homemade whip, to drive the stubborn critters north along the fence trail a couple of miles to

where they might find a bite of something edible which had been overlooked before the feeding period began.

The pep-less cattle were hard to move. They wanted to stick around the water and be spoon-fed. As I poked along, yelling at the cattle and lashing the drags, I saw lightning flashing in the near distance and heard the roll of thunder ever nearer. Glancing over my shoulder I noticed the clouds thicken and come together in violent electric crashes. I wasn't a bit afraid of being caught out in a storm. It had been too long since I had had any intimate knowledge of rain.

But when the wind sprang up I stopped to take notice. The heavy, dark blue clouds were in the south, upriver, and seemed to be moving rapidly in our direction. The cows stopped when I did, and stood motionless on the high, flat ridge about a mile from the windmill, seeming to wait, as I did, for what looked like a sure thing. How could it miss? It was almost up to the south border of our range.

"Come on! Come on!" I shouted hopefully.

I could see the rain pouring down in dark sheets, and smell it, and now and then feel a little lost droplet land on my hand or face. This time it was really coming. . . . But, no, even as I stood in the saddle and leaned to meet it, the storm veered left and rushed off down to the river in a real gully-washer, leaving us high and dry.

I sat back in an agony of frustrated hope and made a fool of myself screaming harsh curses at the indifferent clouds. The trail hugged the wire fence, and I was stopped right beside a thick mesquite post. Crying and yelling at the top of my voice, I hauled off and gave the post a mighty kick. Good heavens! Down it fell flat, having rotted at ground level, and five more tumbled after it like ninepins. In a matter of seconds the ridge was fenceless. The other side belonged to a retired border official who took a dog-in-the-manger attitude about the tall, dry grass that covered that part of his ranch where no cattle of his could run because it was too far from his water facilities. Now, owing to the fury of a strong wind and a woman's kick, his hoarded grass lay unprotected.

The thirty-odd cows and calves and yearlings I had been driving along the bare side of the fence were as astonished as I, but they did not remain long immobile. A cow I called Old Big Dollar — she had a large, round, red spot on her jaw — tentatively stepped over the first wire of the supine fence, then the second, then the third — and there she was where she had been longing to be all summer, in grass up to her knees. In a moment, the rest of the herd were all around her and in front of her, their heads bogged down in grass. It wasn't green grass, but it was headed out and very filling. It would have taken two good cowboys with swinging ropes to whip them back across the fence and prop it up again. And after all, Old Meanie was getting a good rain and my hungry cows had only got tantalized.

For the wealthy, such as my uncompromising neighbor, there are no sure calamities except death and taxes. They need fear no natural disaster — even a long-drawn-out drought. Cattle to them are collateral. They haven't hand-raised them for three or four bovine generations, so individuals don't matter. If a drought hits their range, they can sell their livestock and let the land rest for a comeback. The owner of a purebred Hereford ranch where I buy bulls told me that in thirty years he had dried-up and sold all his cattle on three separate occasions. Or with money enough they can drill deep wells along stream valleys and clear the land and raise adequate feed from irrigated fields. Usually they are ranching for some reason besides making a living: maybe for adventure, or health, or even for business speculation, since western land has appreciated in value at enormous rates in the last decades.

But for us who are in the livestock-raising business the hard way, and must either make it pay or get tin bills and peck with the chickens, there's nothing to it, but to gamble on rain.

What are the odds? What is our average annual rainfall?

A neighbor with a good rain gauge and a range nearer the mountains than mine kept careful account for eight years. According to his records, the best year for volume of measured rain was 1951 with 23.85 inches; the poorest year provided 9.97 inches; the average for the eight years was 17.08 inches.

But as important as the amount that falls is the spacing of the rains. One good year there was only 12.82 inches of rain, yet it was so well spaced that in July he noted: "Grass is as good as I ever saw it this time of year. Plenty of tank water." At the year's end he wrote: "Rained good until September, then turned off dry and did not rain any more. Fair feed, but calves very light." For 1950 he wrote: "Calves fifty pounds light. Water situation terrible." Yet July had given him five inches and started good feed: it was not followed up with August and September showers. His best year for volume he summarized: "Very good grass year. Water situation improved, but not good. Much of rainfall day-by-day light showers quickly evaporating."

The best year for distribution of rainfall had 5.35 inches in July, 2.63 in August, and 2.25 in September. The summary for the year reads: "Very good grass year. Cattle all fat and weighed good. As a whole the best in a good many years." The last year of the record was summed up as: "Most rainfall in July and August that we have on record.

Good grass and water everywhere. But cattle not fat. Insignificant moisture in September, so that the grass did not have the strength to it."

Then came the great drought of 1956, when cattlemen met in distress and petitioned governors to request the U. S. Department of Agriculture to declare disaster areas. The federal government came to our aid. I bought barley for one-third of its price, the USDA paying the remaining two-thirds.

Evidently that year discouraged my neighbor, for the rest of his nice big record book is empty.

Thus it can be seen that "average annual rainfall" in a dry country, as with most other averages, is non-existent. We are supposed to have two rainy seasons a year. Winter-spring lasts from November to April. The summer season, (of late years generally called our Southwestern monsoon period by local newspapers) is July-August-September, and the greatest of these is September. Whatever green growth may have sprung up from early spotted showers will burn to paper-like fibre without the enriching late summer moisture. Our growing season usually lasts well into November in the southern part of the state.

Rain is a touchy subject in this country. In the "spotted showers" season, ranchers meet, and tactfully, sympathetically inquire about each other's rainfall. There are among us some who might be called rain-worshipers, so excessive is our reverence for pennies from heaven. An early September story that once appeared in the *Wickenburg Sun* (a weekly newspaper published in the heart of good Arizona ranch country) led with this paragraph from the typewriter of a reporter who knew his public:

"A marvelous, wonderful, stupendous, colossal and superb storm started pouring rain on the parched earth at

11:30 a.m. Wednesday and continued the downpour for two hours."

All in cow country will now please rise and shout: "Give that feller a Pulitzer prize!" For imaginative and accurate reporting of the news as it deserves to be reported, he merits more than pleasant smiles. I hope the ranchers in his area at least bought him a new hat.

CHAPTER 12

Too Much of a Good Thing

It puzzles me to find so much written on the subject of people bored with their daily lives. It is a cinch such people do not teach school or punch cows. The cowpunching range life — perhaps the least monotonous of all occupations — goes along in a manner that is adventurous, exciting, hazardous, and unpredictable. Day by day, it offers little irresponsible freedom and no unassailable security. When you think you've touched bottom, the bottom falls out.

Ranching is a series of crises. To keep you alert, the animals become ill or get poisoned by noxious weeds or bad water, or fall prey to careless hunters or common thieves. They tumble off cliffs, or get trapped in old mine diggings. When the calves are all on the ground and the cows are doing well, financial troubles and other wide-awake worries can arise with stunning suddenness. They arise from such causes as breakdowns in machinery, accidents, drought, and rain.

Rain?

Can it be that wonderful, life-giving rain can damage anything except cotton plants and the roads in this great canyon-corrugated valley? Rain on the range is the blessing from the sky. It means life instead of starvation; staying with the outfit another year instead of giving up. It is the whole story. Yet in these wild canyons it can be a killer: dumping an overfull cloud that may wipe you out in one flash-flood. Sudden enough and hard enough, it can devastate plain and desert also, as Noah found out. Even in towns and cities in southern Arizona, hardly a year passes that lives aren't lost in raging floods — sometimes within the municipal limits. Innocent-looking arroyos, or dips in highways, become spillways for powerful torrents that sweep cars, and once in awhile houses, right along with their hapless occupants.

The San Pedro River is exceptionally flood-prone. Its tributary channels, numbered by the hundred, are often miles long and are funnel-sided steep gashes in the earth built by floods and for floods. I have ranched in two of these channels. The upshot is that I wouldn't advise it. Experience shows that it seldom rains in a canyon because of down-drafts. "Scattered showers" hit all around on hill and plain. Rains fall on the mesas bordering the river bottom. But when you see a hard rain "washing hell off the cross," as the cowboys say, on the high divide at the head of your canyon, particularly when your place remains dry, look for trouble.

It was time for the rainy season — if any — to begin. We could pump out the well at the upper place in two hours, and it took all night for it to come up again. The cattle hung around the water so that it was impossible to keep the troughs full. We chased them off before feeding time, the Uncle and I, because we could give hay only to those we thought might go down. But the deep-set eyes of hunger are haunting.

At Mesquite Corrals, two miles below the house, the storage was so low that when the pump failed one day there was nothing but black ooze in the long cement *canoa* (feeding trough) and the goldfish died. Hundreds of young quail drowned there trying to drink. It was easy for them to hop down into the canoa, but they couldn't get out again. Each day we rescued a bunch and threw out the dead. Nothing could save them but rain to fill the troughs so they might drink from the brim.

After five bad seasons, hope itself is painful. It hurt to see the white clouds puff up on the horizon the morning of San Juan's Day. Newspapers in southern Arizona co-operate in preserving the tradition that it always rains on San Juan's Day somewhat in the same way as Groundhog Day is publicized in other sections of the country.

At the lower well, deep enough (nearly 300 feet) to hold its water level throughout dry years, the windmill wasn't throwing enough water to keep up with the cattle, so we decided to pull the sucker rods and put new leathers on the cylinder. Wilbur, the friend living in the village who liked to spend Sundays out in the open, and another fellow not long from Texas who had a box of tools and a good set of chain blocks, came out to do the work.

Arturo was the schoolboy vacationing on the ranch that year. Shortly after midday he and I drove the five miles down the canyon to take lunch to the men. They were hot and tired and dirty, but they wouldn't eat until they had finished the job. Wilbur, an Arizonan, didn't say anything about the clouds, or the wind that was springing up, but Tex remarked that if he were in God's country, he'd say it was going to rain. Speaking about rain before it arrives is taboo around here. Always when he left the house, the Old Vaquero said: "Leave my bed outside. If it gets wet I like it that way." When it began to sprinkle and I ran out to take in the wash or the bedclothes from the cots, the Uncle would say: "You'll scare it away."

That day, in less time than it took to eat a sandwich, the western sky rapidly mobilized into barrages of light-ning and thunder and the strong wind began to mean business. We broke up our picnic lunch and prepared to leave in a rush.

The cloud burst over Rice Peak, right at the head of Pepper Sauce Canyon, and that meant water in the well for the house again. It could also mean a flood that could fill the whole canyon.

Wilbur and Arturo elected to ride the horses over the ridge trail to drive Utah, an old cholla-eater, and her calf to the feed corrals above. Tex and I threw the stuff into Wilbur's car and made a dash up the wash for safety — a five-mile race against the oncoming waters. I knew if we didn't reach the road to the ranch before it washed out, we would be cut off from home for no telling how long. I knew, too, that beating the flood through the last two miles of box-walled canyon meant survival itself.

Tex kept griping at my reckless haste, arguing that he could tell by the waterline along the cliffs that the water never got more than a foot deep, so what if we did meet a flood? I ignored his plainsman's comments to concentrate on making speed and watching the rain gather and come straight at us. Halfway up the "Box" we found the water running down the ruts and spreading over the sand. Even so, we had to stop a moment and frantically chase a cow and her calf out from under a little tree and up the ridge trail.

By the time we reached the small gorge where the road is cut to lead up to the house, the water was over the floorboards and I had my door unlatched, ready to abandon ship. Reaching the safety of the forty-acre ledge on the ridge above the canyon wall, we splashed ankle-deep across a river to get to the door of the main cabin. All depressions on both hillsides were running full and emptying pell-mell into the main stream. As I struggled with window sashes and flapping screens, sure enough, I heard, above the noise of the drumming downpour on the low roof, the wild, continuous roar of the flood. It was impossible to resist running to the edge of the bank to see it.

Old Tex stared open-mouthed into the dark, tumbling cataract. Where we had driven up the sand-wash on a well-packed road minutes before, a four-foot wall of water roared down the canyon bank-to-bank. Seeing was believing. He swore in wonder.

It was the biggest flood I had seen there in seven years' occupancy. Grandma Pierson, who lived on Mesquite Wash, the largest tributary of Pepper Sauce, said that in thirty-five years she had never seen bigger. Where Mesquite joined the main canyon, the murky rushing water, taking everything before it, was a thousand feet wide. It ran all the way to the San Pedro River, thirteen miles away, wiping out roads and fences, and changing channel beds.

Even as we stood in the soaking rain watching the great washout, Tex began to moan about how was he going to get back to the village, twelve miles over hill and canyon, to be with his new (middle-aged) wife whom he had never been away from a single night. He couldn't possibly not get home, he declared. I wasn't interested. My exultation over the rain had begun to dim as I watched the pasture fence go by. Worry intensified as I saw waves tentatively lap over the stone embankment that protected the well. That well, covered by a rude tin shack, with a new engine and the two miles of pipeline down the canyon, was the heart and arteries of the ranch. The Uncle's breakwater, meshed with hog wire, slowly began to come apart on the lower end. The water rose in spurts on the sides of the flimsy wellhouse.

The deafening flood, rank with the sweepings of long drought, cut its way down the curving walls of the canyon and hit the opposite bank at the big turn with the force of a Niagara. The backwash eddied up around the big cottonwood tree and reached the area of the well, carrying off the fifty-gallon gasoline barrel (just filled) and the five-gallon oil can. The next thing to go would be the new engine, not yet fully paid for. Then the well would fill up with sand and trash. I stared at the sky for signs of respite and hope. Just as the near side of the well-house swung loose at the bottom giving the flood a cleaner swipe at the boards that covered the well curbing, the climax was reached. With sputtering claps of thunder and a few light dashes of belated raindrops, San Juan called off his waterspout.

Two hours later I was able to wade across to the well to survey the damage. Most of the wrenches, pipes, and small tools had gone with the gasoline and oil drums. A thick smear of slimy silt covered the wellhouse floor and the stout wooden cover that protected the precious well, but the well itself was still intact although its water would be red with fine silt for several days. The flood had just reached the two-by-sixes that held the engine in place.

A few days later, we found the full gasoline barrel wedged in some mesquite roots several feet above the creek bed half a mile below the house. As far as we knew, only one cow had drowned: the Hunting Neighbor found her swollen body several miles below the Windmill.

The greatest damage done was to the pipeline. We had laid it along the edges of the creek bed and covered it with a foot or two of sand and rocks. It had withstood the ravages of seven years of summer floods, but this one got it. Human labor above and beyond the call of good sense and discretion finally disclosed that for a quarter of a mile where the canyon was most narrow, the line was broken into joints; many of them twisted or broken, all of them packed solid with mud, and buried under tons of recently soaked sand.

Over the years we had noticed that some floods cleaned out the sand, leaving the creek-bed full of unwieldy boulders; others brought in enormous quantities of new sand, loose and hard to travel by automobile. This flood was the champion in the latter category. We had to work our way down the canyon by practically paving the road ruts with brush and stones. What surely must have been the entire supply of sand on the east slopes of the Santa Catalina Mountains had been dumped on our broken pipeline. For two hot days of fruitless digging, we couldn't even find a trace of it. The Uncle cut a forked stick from a peach tree and "witched," but since the pipes were filled with sand instead of water, he got no results. We rode the canyon in careful search without finding a length of pipe, but there was no question of giving up. We had to find that pipeline and fix it or the best part of our range would not be usable for lack of drinking water.

With shovels, and crowbars to pry the rocks, the Uncle, Arturo, and I cut an exploratory ditch all the way across the canyon at a bend a few hundred yards below the well. There, at the depth of four feet, we found a couple of lengths of pipe. All that digging in heavy wet sand had us exhausted. A bulldozer was in order, but for us it was as out of the question as the Uncle's wish for a scraper and a team of mules. At the village I found a couple of men who kindly consented to come out and dig. Once committed, nobody quit. To this day I marvel at the fortitude and generosity of those who did all that terrible digging under a hot July sun for the end purpose of putting water for the cattle at the lower watering troughs at "Mesquite" and "Dos Pilitas."

The Old Vaquero had gone to the mountain to cut

wood for the vacationers as he did every summer when I could not pay him wages. He heard of our disaster and rode down the mountain to throw his strength — in his prime it had been that of two good men — into the Herculean job of digging ditches in the heavy, damp sand for hundreds of yards, to a depth, in places, of *ten feet*. I could not pay him or the Uncle or Arturo any money, and I am ashamed to say I paid the "hired" men only $2.50 a day plus transportation. But everybody was game. I fed them well on biscuits, refried beans, jerky gravy, and chocolate cake, and dug along beside them.

In less than a week the job was done — the pipes found, mended, cleaned out, and connected — and we were pumping water into the lower troughs. In another week we could make the road up and down the sand-wash without getting stuck, and the fences were back in place. By that time, the tender green grass and weeds that had come out after the heavy rain were scorched to the ground. It was nineteen days before it rained another drop.

In volume, that was the biggest flood that ever struck my outfit, but it was not the most costly. Top rating in that class goes to the Great Flood suffered here in this canyon, July 13, 1955 — a disaster that took the lives of nine head of cattle and put my water system out of commission for many days. What made it extra hard to bear was that out of that storm, terrific up on the high divide, we didn't get a drop here on the ranch. That is why the cattle drowned. They were ambushed by a sudden unexpected wall of water before they were aware of danger.

In summer the cows generally graze on the hills and ridges early in the morning. They then bring their calves and yearlings down to the creek to drink and lie in the shade near the water until the cool of the evening, when they slowly climb out again in search of food. But as soon as it starts to rain or snow, they hurry off to a high place. If they didn't, there wouldn't be any cattle left in this treacherous gorge we inhabit for the sake of the water it furnishes. Practically all canyons on the west side of the steep mountains and foothills that rim the San Pedro Valley on the east are death traps. Several miles south of us at Clark Wash a few summers ago, my neighbors, the Mercers, lost twenty-four head of cattle in a big rise that came down on the unsuspecting creatures lying in the dry shade of a high bluff near the surface water where they were wont to drink. That rain cost the owners over $2000 — and cost the cattle their lives.

Nature endows a cow with instinct enough to get out of low places when it starts to rain. But she doesn't give it sense enough to look up the creek and see a big storm that will send a wall of water, armed with logs and uprooted trees and giant boulders, on a drive down the canyon into places that are still deceptively dry. Cows are endowed with four life-preserving senses. (Discount *taste:* they often eat things that kill them.) They can *see* danger, and *hear* it, and *smell* it, and *feel* it; but they can't imagine it when it is several miles away.

That accounts for the perishing in the Great Flood of my three young cows and their little calves and the dry cow and two weaned heifer yearlings. They were minding their own business in the dry shade of a mesquite thicket when a juggernaut born of a deluge up on the eastern divide came down with ambush tactics and overwhelming force and swept them out of this life. I had been up the canyon in the Jeep that afternoon and had seen them quietly taking their siestas. I never saw them again. There was a lazy old fat bull with the bunch, and I figured that he, too, had drowned, for we could not find him in any of his regular haunts. Two months later I rode up to a neighbor's water trough and there was my bull making himself at home with the neighbor's cows. He had escaped the flood, but it scared him so much that he left his own country and emigrated to a safer land.

Fortunately, we are near enough to the high mountains to get at least a few warning drops when a flood is imminent. Otherwise all our cattle would die, as most of them drink from living water in the creek bed. One favorite cow, Little Tita, drowned right when it was raining. When the flood caught her on one side of the creek and her three-month-old calf on the other, maternal anxiety compelled her to plunge into the dark torrent.

One summer evening I raced a flood down to the spring in the old Jeep pickup. We had seen a shower up in the high country; but I could look right through it and see the mountains, so I was convinced there was no danger of flood. Neighbor Pete who lives alone two miles up the canyon at the non-producing mines and comes down to help with the chores and share our evening meal, was worried about his well. It is located in the creek bed near one bank, and has a cement curbing about four feet in height to protect it. A good-sized flood will go over the top and fill it with rocks and muck. Usually he keeps it tightly covered, but he had been cleaning it out and deepening it because of the falling water level during the dry season. He was practically a newcomer and therefore he relied on my judgment that there would be no flood and that it was safe to stay for supper. He had walked down, so I sent Jesús to take him home in the Jeep. Jesús (pronounced Hay-soós) was a young Mexican whom I had helped to immigrate. He came to help me for a few months while the Old Vaquero was off somewhere taking quack treatments for his arthritis.

In a few minutes, Jesús came running to the corral to

find me, crying excitedly: "There's a big flood coming down the canyon. It is at the Iron Gate now."

The trouble was that we had just started the pump. It is situated a mile away from the house, on the far side of the canyon where there is a fairly high ledge of rock-ribbed land on which to anchor it above the spring. If we should leave it running during a flood, the muddy water would jimmy its works, besides putting foul sediment in the storage tank here at the house.

Away we went on a wild ride down the terrible road, I hanging on to the wheel and Jesús clutching at whatever he could grab. Around the sharp bends and across the deep arroyos and over the ruts and boulders and tire-cutting sharp rocks we raced in second gear, doing our dangedest. Luckily, our dangedest was enough.

We leaped out at the creek bank and heard the mighty rumbling coming around the bend like an express train a few yards above us.

"Run, Jesús!" I cried, tossing him my flashlight.

Jesús ran. In seconds he made the rocky creek bed and the level stretch, pulled the sparkplug cord, and dashed back to safety, the roaring flood lapping at his heels.

The sound of it, the smell of it, the sight of it — like nothing else on earth — held us stupefied. We stood speechless at its edge, my light searching for casualties, although I was pretty sure that no cattle had been caught, for they do not sleep in the creek bottom at night. Too many rocks.

My light followed the dark, foam-flecked waves as they rolled over the crystal-clear spring beneath the overhanging bluff. In the early years, I used to worry about flood damage to the spring. All the fortifications — high cement walls, concrete boxes, and four-inch iron pipes — were swept away as fast as we could set them up. But we have learned that the spring, like hope, seems eternal. Centuries of floods have not destroyed it. It fights back, gently and persistently; and when the fury of the flood has passed, it finds its way through sand and stone, through all the outrageous debris, to bubble up to the surface in a fountain of delight.

CHAPTER 13

Cooking for Cattle

The word is *cholla.* We pronounce it *chóya,* because the double "l" is a letter in the Spanish alphabet, having the sound of "y." It is cactus of the prickliest kind, sometimes called "jumping" because of its facility for sticking you when you're not looking. Belonging to our Southwestern desert originally, it is widespread now, I am told, in Australia, South America, and other lands.

In dry and hard times, when I go out to burn chollas, loaded down with paraphernalia, I tramp the steep trails in the twilight to the rhythm of the lines from Stephen Vincent Benét: "Fire on the mountains—snakes in the grass. Satan's here a bilin'—Oh, Lordy, let him pass!"

Behind me, following in long, uneven columns, like the children after the Pied Piper, is a line of hungry cows, heifers, calves, and a few bulls. The cattle know I am going out to the only crop left on the place to prepare a meal for them, and they bring along good appetites for the singed cactus. Burning chollas is not easy labor. I do it simply to keep the cattle alive and functioning; and even so I do it only in the last extremity.

The last extremity means that the rains didn't come; there is nothing to eat on the range. The grass — what was left of it — has been scorched to pale, dry ash. The browse is tough and bitter. The desperate cattle are trying to eat the raw cholla — bundles of juicy, gray-green pods

150

encased in masses of whitish inch-long spines as stiff and dangerous as fishhooks. Indeed, like fishhooks, they have little guards at the tip so that they are difficult to yank out of flesh.

When the cows have tried to eat the pods, they come in to water at the corrals unable to eat or drink, their mouths and noses pincushions of white stickers, inside and out. They twist their heads, trying to swig up water in spite of the torturous appendages. I take them on one at a time in a game of "dodge," springing around each critter to get a good swipe at the nose with a long piece of dried sahuaro rib, while she does her best to evade me. Those that have cholla spines inside the mouth, between the lips, or cover-ing — sometimes even piercing — an eye, I must rope and tie to the snubbing post while I work on them with long-nosed pliers.

The cattle, of course, don't understand what is happen-ing. They turn away stunned, perhaps as much with dumb surprise as with distress. All they had wanted was the "apple," the round juicy fruit of the cholla, of which they are very fond. I have eaten them myself when far from water on a hot day. They are watery with a lemon taste. You peel them carefully, minding the tiny stickers, then chew them up and spit out the seeds, which are practically indestructible — no seed ever had more protection.

When it becomes plain during a drought that my cows are reduced to a diet of cactus, I go out in the *chollales* (cholla thickets) and commence Operation Burn. Previ-ously I will have gone to the village, stocked up on extra kerosene and matches, and on the way home stopped in the vast cholla flats to load the pickup with seasoned stalks of dead cholla knocked down years before by windstorms, or killed by grass fires. These stalks make excellent torches. I pick them long and well dried so they won't weigh much, for I must hold one as a lighted torch in my right hand while carrying a can of kerosene in my left. The innumerable perforations in the trunk of the cholla serve as built-in bellows, and provide perfect ventilation for the blaze. The fibrous wood is strong, yet almost as easy to fire as paper.

When I speak of burning cholla, I do not mean burning live cactus, which would be like trying to burn millions of capsules full of water. In fact I've often remarked that a good way to stop a big fire would be to dump tons of live cholla on it. Even though you can put a match to one and have it flare up like a rocket of flame, the cholla remains as good as ever, with plenty of unburned stickers. The method is to apply a strong blaze to the stubborn spines long enough to singe or soften them — count ten before you move your torch — so the cattle can eat the pods in comfort. To use a common expression, they are crazy about them, especially while they are hot.

In cold weather the burning can be done in daylight hours, if other chores are not too pressing. During the long hot summertime you can stand it only at night — when you have to be on the watch for snakes and red ants and the cactus all over the ground, just waiting for a chance to stab you on the ankles. While the drought was on in 1960-61, I personally burned cholla for over two hundred nights, not missing over half a dozen during all that time, and then only because of drizzles of rain or snow. It's quite a sight to see a cholla "tree" — some are taller than a man on horseback — blazing skyward while snowflakes are falling, the huddling cows minding neither flame nor ice crystals, but chomping steadily away for dear life.

In my years of cowpunching in a tough country I have become a Jenny-of-all-trades, but expert in only two: driving a car uphill in deep sand, and burning cholla. This burning is no snap. As with all skills, it takes experience.

All right, Junior, here's your dry cholla stick. Dip the end in kerosene, put a match to it, touch it to that big fat cholla tree, and stand back. See the exploding fire rush through and around and up in a rising upside-down cascade of roaring flame. Watch the burning particles fall to the ground and spread like flaming gas through the rat's nest and other debris piled up under the cholla. Feel the heat! See how bright it is! But even as you look, the raging fire is gone — vanished in thirty seconds or less.

Now take your torch and examine a few hundred of the myriad pods on that cholla. Find one whose stickers are entirely burned away so that a cow can put it into her mouth. You see? Not one!

Now, let's get to work. You take that side of the tree and I'll take this. Let us move slowly over each branch, burning away all the spines that escaped the first fire. Take particular care with the very ends of each cholla pod. They have extra moisture which makes them fire-resistant and able to root wherever they hit the ground. It is at this point that the cow's lips and tongue first touch the reached-for morsel.

As with most interesting cookery, this cannot be done in a hurry. One night two wetbacks lodged at the ranch, and went out to the chollas with us just as railroad hoboes used to go to the woodpile. Inexperienced, they used up the best torchsticks and inordinate amounts of kerosene and energy, while running swiftly over the ridge-side firing up a storm. They made a great show. Next morning after they had left I spent hours — after shutting the cows in the corral until I had finished preparing their repast — reburning the big area they had only half done.

Years ago there was a movement afoot to import a bug from Australia that would destroy cholla and nothing else. Cowmen had tried various methods to eradicate them from the ranges. A wealthy land owner hired two tractors to travel through his cholla flats side by side with a heavy chain between, to knock down the plants. (I don't know what he did to keep every joint that hit the ground from taking root. They do.) The agricultural scientists experimented with injecting poison — probably arsenic — into the plants, which of course killed the plants and also killed every creature that fed on them. Cattlemen have tried letting the grass grow high, and when frost and drought have dehydrated it, setting it on fire. On a windy day, that will burn the chollas enough to give them a few years' setback. It will also burn all the yucca and mesquite, palo verde, and *nopal,* leaving parched earth wide open to erosion.

A neighbor gave me a scare with one of these disaster measures. About midday in a high wind some friends from the village drove excitedly into my yard yelling: "A forest fire is headed this way!" Forest? We are miles from any forest. Nevertheless I knew what they meant: a range fire, sending smoke billowing high into the sky above the enclosing ridges.

The Vaquero, who had seen everything in his fifty-odd years on the range, happened to be here at the time. Under his direction, we grabbed shovels and wet gunnysacks, and canteens of water for ourselves, and rushed off to fight the fire. It had started on a promontory-like ridge jutting out between two deep canyons, bristling with cholla so thick you couldn't ride through them; but it had ridden the wind off that ridge and started up the slope of the road ridge, which had no cholla on that side but was covered with dry grass, yucca, bushes, and prickly pear — all good forage. It was a hot fire and traveling fast. The villagers and I, watching the Vaquero, threw down our shovels and wet sacks and copied his method, cutting a branch from a mesquite and using it as a broom to sweep the flames back into the blackened area. In two hours of furious labor we surrounded the fire, stopping it a few hundred yards before it reached my fence. I took pride in the big favor we had done my neighbor.

Later, of course, I learned he had purposely set the fire, since the wind was right, to burn down the cactus jungle.

He gave me another good fright when he dropped matches into a cholla thicket on his side of the fence near the boundary line. I topped the western rim of the wide, deep valley on my way home from the city and looked across to the foothills to see a column of gray smoke coming from the exact direction of my house. Needless to say, I split the breeze for home, breaking a spring on the pickup in my haste, and was relieved to find the fire burning itself out on the ridge above the house!

Considering these efforts to rid the range of cholla, one might think we'd all be glad to have the government import the Australian bugs to eat it up. But the organized cattle growers' vote was negative. Too many ranchers had been reduced to feeding cholla in hard times.

Be that as it is, feeding cactus is strictly a drought measure to be resorted to when other resources are exhausted. As has been said, it is tedious and hazardous work. But there are compensations. It is heartening to see the cattle contentedly and comfortably chomping their suppers. And fire, controlled, is always fascinating. In the spring the pink cholla blossoms look beautiful in the glowing flames. They do not burn when the stickers do, and the smart cows grab for them first. The night air is refreshing after the day's heat. The stars are in their glory. We take recesses to drink cold lemonade and watch for airplanes and satellites moving across the sky. If there are young people present, I show them the constellations and teach them the zodiac.

City folks, incidentally, like cholla wood. They like to gather the dried trunks and branches, and bleach, polish, and varnish them to make table lamps and picture frames to sell to tourists who are intrigued by the peculiar wood. A young German geologist who once came to the ranch was fascinated by the stored pile of cholla sticks, and even begged a piece to send back to Germany. Personally, I can't see the appeal. Cholla plants have caused me too much misery, and I wouldn't have a scrap of the stuff in my house.

CHAPTER 14

The Wide Open Spaces Just Ain't!

There was a place on the old road to the homestead (a few miles out from the village of Oracle) where, after many close turns and narrow passages through thick oaks and granite dells, you suddenly topped a clear rise above the trees and buttes and broken ridges, and had an overwhelming view of the thousand or more square miles of the great San Pedro River Valley, as it slopes gently downward fifteen miles to the river, and then upward in giant steps of mesas and ridges and foothills for twenty-five miles to the multi-colored Galiuro range that forms the Valley's eastern wall.

In the twenty-one years I traveled the winding road, I called that spot the Edge of the World because of the long view dimming off to the distant blue and purple and rose of the mountains to the north and east and south. It was like overlooking one of the widest expanses of the Grand Canyon, except that it is a much broader and, as human history goes, older canyon.

The best hour for the view was sundown, when the slanting light rays would strike precipices and escarpments with an unforgettable glow, and purple dusk filled the valley between. Clouds, with infinite diversity of light and shadow, bestowed an added beauty. In winter, snow-capped rims gave an effect of remoteness. In lucky summers, rain showers, sometimes several at once — laced the otherwise sunlit valley. Moonlight vested it with a cold, unearthly look. And no darkness could shut out the feel of empty windswept distance: empty of human life and its paraphernalia — empty of any life whatsoever. So it always seemed.

A totally wrong impression. All that appearance of emptiness is an illusion. No terrain in the world — not even a rain forest — could be more densely supplied, unit for unit, with inhabitants, both plant and animal.

The hard-bitten plant life forever embattled against heat and dehydration, is readily visible, however modestly it blends into the background. On my Edge of the World you are out of the oaks and manzanitos, entering into mesquites and catclaws and other low bushes and the ubiquitous *amole* and *palmilla* (soapweed and beargrass). Descend a mile or two and you are in yucca country, amid Spanish bayonet and *sotoles* (desert spoons). Here, except in the arroyos, the mesquites are dwarfed and there is a smattering of cactuses — the low-on-the-ground varieties, and stunted cholla and barrel cactus. Farther down the sloping mesas, the chollas get taller and thicker and are interspersed with sahuaros. As the elevation lowers even more, not much grows but greasewood and the tenacious mesquite — desert trees that come into their own in the bottomlands where their roots delve down into underground streams, and their branches form an almost impenetrable thicket for miles up and down the river.

What are invisible, except for a stray now and then that streaks across the road ahead of you, are the fauna — the denizens that live in and on and under every plant.

At a distance, the scene looks today much as it must have looked to the early Spanish explorers or their predecessors. Well, not quite. Progress same into the Valley a few years ago to unearth copper-bearing ores. The only sign of its mighty onslaught visible from the old road is the snout of a 500-foot smelter smokestack, blowing smudgy puffs into the sky like an underground demon not angry enough to belch fire and brimstone. It does little to give the beholder a feeling of nearing "civilization." From this west side of the river, the panorama looks as uninhabited as the moon.

I said "looks." Actually it is teeming with life. Start a home out there on the landscape — any kind of shelter from a tin shack or adobe hut to a split-level mansion, and you'll find you've located among hundreds of millions of flying, creeping, crawling, clawing, ambling creatures — all house-hungry.

These wild-life natives try to move in with you, and never give up. You and your descendants may fight them for generations. They will outlast any warfare made upon them with sprays, guns, or bombs. One need feel no uneasiness about the extinction of creatures of the desert and semi-desert country. They'll be here forever. Light a lamp. Ten thousand flying things will invade and conquer. Leave an unblocked opening. Some curious animal, domestic or wild, will stick his nose in. Sit down in the shade, miles from anywhere, to rest a moment and refresh yourself with an apple or a handful of raisins. Presto! You fight for your life. Start out horseback some damp summer morning, and swarms of enemies will attack your eyes and ears and those of your pony.

Glancing across the seemingly serene landscape, I know that every acre of it has been fought over by the earthly creatures generally considered to be the highest form of life. First they fought with sticks and stones, tomahawks and bowie knives, and early American rifles. Later, as land-hunters, they fought by legal procedure, and with influence over land boards and commissioners. There is not a small ridge, dry mesa, cholla flat, rocky hilltop, or sand-bottomed wash that is not part of some cattle grower's range.

It is sobering — even depressing — to know that on every foot of the ground within my view, living creatures are struggling to the utmost to keep alive, and chances are against them all the way. I think first, naturally, of the cattle. There are, perhaps, thousands in this area — under the trees and bushes, and on the distant grassy slopes near the mountains, lying in shaded canyons, or roaming the cactus flats and ridges. There must be hundreds of range horses out there also. Living beside them and to some extent competing with them for the sparse supplies of foods — even, now and then, preying on these domestic animals for food itself — are the untold thousands of wildlife.

Ranchers are of two minds about wildlife. Most of us enjoy the sight and proximity of such harmless creatures as deer, rabbits, and songbirds. The Uncle spent several dollars a month of his pension money to buy scratch feed for the birds that came to eat with his chickens. "My ole quails," he'd say affectionately, ready to fight any shotgun hunter who came within sight and sound.

As for the carnivores, large and small, that seem to thrive in our far-off country, the general rule is to kill on sight. And this presents its own problems.

Take badgers. They don't harm big animals and they can't climb trees and roosts to get the chickens. But they dig. They dig around fence posts and barn uprights to get at the bugs. The result is a flattened fence or damaged barn. One took up at my place and excavated disastrously — undermining the little hay barn. One morning Jesús snared her with a length of baling wire looped like a rope and dragged her, protesting, to the house. "Where's the gun?" he asked. I viewed her plight with sympathy, and thought of a plan. Jesús sat on the spare tire and held her securely, under a box, while I drove five miles down the road and bade him turn her free. On my way to town a day or two later I met her plodding along the road heading back to my barn.

Badgers are cute creatures. Cal's niece Ruth, an Eastern girl on a visit to the ranch, was delighted with the mother and young'un (exactly like her but half the size) we met on the road. The mother knew about cars and rushed out of the way. The young one ignored her nudge and stood his ground, staring right back at us as we stopped the pickup to watch. Excitedly the mother ran on and off the road and around her baby, but he wouldn't mind. Desperately she darted out; grabbed him by the nape, and literally dragged him away, and for as long as we could see, the mother was still forcefully lugging the heedless brat.

My choice for a merciful end to animals that must die is a well-aimed gun. Traps and poison are blots on humanity's record. I once met a strychnined coyote in the canyon, crawling on his belly to get to water. His suffering was so appalling that I can never forget it.

Some cowmen — not all — say that coyotes kill calves. If they have a good chance, if no cow is baby-sitting, or if an orphan is left undefended, probably so. But in all my experience I have never, as far as I know, lost an animal to coyotes.

I have told the trappers they cannot set traps on any land that I control. One did anyway. I found a miserable coyote trapped by the roadside in my narrow canyon. I killed him for mercy's sake — he was in bad shape — and confiscated the trap. I threw it and two other identical steel torture machines in the river. The Uncle worried. "They'll git you for that," he warned. "It's the same as stealing."

"It's not anything that I want or need," I defended. "Taking property is illegal, yes. But inflicting prolonged pain on helpless animals hunting for food is a worse crime." We both knew the lazy trapper sometimes didn't check his trapline for a week.

Of course the Uncle was unconvinced, but when he set out little traps for skunks around the chicken house, he watched them carefully after that.

One summer ten-year-old Preston, living up the creek, had a neighbor boy a few years older for a pal. But it hurt Preston to find that the older boy liked to kill small things like birds and squirrels. He set out baited traps — he had a dozen or more made of steel — for the little rock squirrels. They weren't good to eat and he wasn't hungry; it was simply fun for him to catch the small things and kill them. Preston, skillful with rocks, told me how he watched his chance and threw rocks to hit the paddles and spring the traps. The other boy's family moved away suddenly leaving the traps. Preston gathered them up, and we threw them over a fall where the floods would wash them away.

Although small birds are often irresistible targets for stone-throwing, slingshot-wielding boys, in the first year at Redington School I had a good chance to indoctrinate the children in a different kind of feeling toward little birds. We wrote stories, tried to draw pictures of, and were very fond of a little nesting bird whom we named Elsie. She had made a nest in the top of the supply cupboard, having entered through a broken pane of glass in the school door. We looked up Elsie in a library book which gave her the unromantic classification of *flycatcher.* And we thought ours was the only school in the United States chosen by a wild bird to raise a family in.

The thorn in the rose was that we couldn't repair the broken glass until she and her young had flown away, and she wasn't the only flying thing that liked our quarters.

Wasps! Sunday afternoon before the opening day, I found the tongue-and-groove ceiling of the classroom chandeliered with a dozen or more wasps' nests of assorted sizes, all occupied. I ran down to the teacherage for the Flit gun, and with persistence, swept out all their summer architecture with the dust. Next morning, school or no school, they were back and had started rebuilding.

Wasps are pushy. Wherever they can find an opening in a man-made building, they make themselves at home. As I write, my forearm is swollen and itchy from a sting received this morning in the hay shed down in the horse trap. I reached up to pull down a bale of hay when *zoom* came a yellow-jacket — a stab of pain barbed with long-lasting irritants! Retaliating, I came to the house for an empty can, half-filled it with gasoline, and returned to give the wasps a fatal dousing. One splash of gasoline and it was all over with Mrs. Wasp and family.

In the stretch of country visible from my High Point, if it were possible to take count of the insects and crawling pests dwelling therein, the sum would exceed the national debt plus the miles between earth and sun and all the other stars. The best insects I can think of are bees, butterflies, and ladybugs. The worst are scorpions, black widows, tarantulas, burning worms, and bellows bugs — also known as "Hualapai tigers," or, in Spanish, *chinches.*

Only the scorpions and black widows are deadly and they only rarely, to a feeble person or a child. The scorpion in my foothills and canyons is one of the deadly varieties — a small greenish-yellow one. Look out for these scorpions when you pick up a board from a pile of lumber, or a mesquite post, or a stick of firewood, or when you turn over a good-sized rock. They live in houses, too; especially those made of wood or adobe, and seem able to swim through the water traps in sinks and bathtubs. They lie in wait in towels hanging on the wall, or crawl into your shoes at night. When the main cabin of my homestead was new, I could turn on the flashlight any night and see four or five scorpions scooting up the mud walls. The thing to do was to grab the hammer by the bedside and give each one a good smash. To date, I have been stung twenty-two times, thereby probably developing a degree of immunity so that it hurts for only six or eight hours.

When it first happened to me, the pain, the numbness, the tongue and throat thickness, and the strange inertia lasted for sixteen hours — perhaps prolonged by fright. Ice seems to help more than anything. It slows the circulation so that the body can cope better with the poison as it spreads, and it relieves the pain, too. But even ice can do nothing for a tarantula bite. The victim twists and squirms for hours — in my case, seven. The Italian dance, "La Tarantella," is not idly named. Such pain could not be borne in relaxation.

In our southwestern cities, for all the pavement, brick, and stone blocks and last word marvels of housebuilding, there must be constant war on pests such as ants, termites, cockroaches, silverfish, ticks, fleas, flies, gnats, scorpions, centipedes, and even tarantulas — not to mention such destructive little creatures as crickets and mice. There are thriving companies whose business is pest control. And occasionally our newspapers run stories about a housewife having called the police to help get a rattlesnake off her porch, or a skunk out of her garage.

At Redington I had the nicest teacherage in the county. One of the ranch owners was a city banker who had remade an old two-room adobe into a pleasant cottage he could occupy when visiting the ranch. It was my good luck to inherit it as a fringe benefit of the job. It rested on the edge of a steep-sided mesa overlooking the river bottom, commanding a fine view of the cottonwoods and mesquite thickets and the blue mountains to the west. In front of the two rooms, which had no connecting door, a long, narrow screened-in porch had been added, and behind them, a six-by-six kitchen and a little bathroom. The hillside sloped so abruptly, that while the kitchen-bath sat squarely on the ground, the porch entrance was a steep three-step flight above it, and the room where I slept — and "lived," since it had a fireplace — was on a stone foundation from four to two feet high. This arrangement made a nice basement apartment for wildlife.

The place was well aged and long inhabited before I moved in. I stuffed wads of newspaper into the gaping spaces around the window and door frames to keep out the mice. A few skinny lizards slithered in now and then, but since they parked strategically on the worn screens to catch flies and moths, they were welcome. Not so the big rattlesnake that somehow climbed up the porch steps and a panel or two of the old door, and got in through a gap in the screen.

I did not fire up the chimney in the bed-living room except in the evenings. Mornings, still in pajamas, I dashed out along the porch and into the second room, where I had a trigger-fast iron stove, a dining table, and a mirror over a chest of drawers near the clothes rack. There I dressed, and ate the breakfast prepared over a two-burner kerosene stove in the kitchen.

One chilly fall morning I threw some waste paper into the stove and went back on the porch for some kindling I had stored in a shallow wooden box. The wonderful view of the autumn-touched cottonwoods against the blue mountains held my gaze. Suddenly my groping fingers encountered a strange surface. I looked down, and there, her unmistakable head in the exact center of the diamondback coils, lay a rattlesnake, sound asleep in the chip box. I put on a robe, tied up my hair, propped open the screen-door, and gently picked up the box. Carefully, I tiptoed across the long porch and down the steep hill to the Big House, and roused the family. Quicker than speech, the men snatched me away from the box. Out dumped my nice kindling and the dangerous intruder.

The ranch had a special attraction for snakes. They were around the corrals, along the trails, across the roads, in the buildings. The children were trained to watch for them every step. At one time the great house had been a dude ranch. During that period it had been added to, and divided up in surprising ways. At the end of a long passage only three feet wide, a two and one-half-foot door opened into a tiny enclosure holding a convenience. I was in the kitchen visiting with Lavita, woman of the house, mother of little cowpunchers, when we heard desperate shrieks from Grandma. We dashed through the house and down the passage, and yanked her to safety. A huge rattlesnake, hanging from a hole in the wall on a level with a sitter's head, was fast disappearing into a deep crack. I grabbed the tail and held on against amazing strength while Lavita ran for a weapon. It was all I could do, might and main, to jerk her out to the floor, where we killed her with the hoe.

During the second year of my tenancy, the big hideaway under my front rooms became winter quarters for a rattler that measured, when she emerged months later, five feet in length. I discovered her late in November, at the end of a cloudy, windy day. The storm that had been threatening for hours struck a little while after school was dismissed. I had stood out on the porch to watch it approach in a great display of lightning and thunder and a fury of wind that sent the cottonwood leaves swirling in all directions. When the slanting rain threatened to drench me, I went inside and lay on the bed under an army blanket.

All at once a terrific crash of thunder shook the whole house. Above its dying rumble sounded the unmistakable rattling. It seemed right in the room with me. I couldn't lie there, and I didn't dare get up. Cautiously I raised up and dug out the flashlight from under my pillow. There was nothing under the bed but my boots. I picked them up and put them on. Slowly my light-beam raked over every foot of the floor. Nothing was there. Yet each vibration from thunder set off the rattling. I began to realize that the snake must be under the floor. Nevertheless, I sat up on the bed, flashlight alerted, until the storm let up and atmospheric serenity reigned again.

When I started to walk across the room, the rattling started once more. But I was bold, for I realized that almost half an inch of old flooring protected me. I stamped about until I cornered the snake in a northeast nook of the room, under the typewriter table near the apple box bookcases. There she had dug in for the winter and she was safe. There was no way to get at her without taking up the floor; nobody had money enough for that enterprise.

The situation provided an unusual opportunity for nature study. The first thing I learned was that the way to make her angry was to click the keys of the typewriter. When I started typing she went into a furious buzzing that never failed to make me jerk my feet up on the chair. Knowing I was stuck with the rattler until such time as she voluntarily departed, I was tempted to share my startling experience with others. I squelched the impulse to rush down to the Big House with my news, and awaited developments. After supper, when Delbert, Lavita's young brother-in-law, came up to listen to Amos and Andy on my battery-powered radio, I waited until he was comfortably sprawled in a chair and absorbed in the program, then casually turned to the little typewriter and began: "Now is the time . . ." and laughed like a fool when he hit the ceiling.

When he was convinced that nothing could be done — short of tearing the place apart — he connived with me, with a cowboy's natural turn for practical joking, to play the trick on others. Never a visiting cowboy or linerider or horse trader or cattle buyer dropped by the ranch for the night that Delbert didn't inveigle him into calling on the teacher.

Of course I told Lavita and the children about my snake, and all of them, even the bus riding pupils, came for a demonstration. Nobody was disappointed. The rattler never developed patient acceptance of the clicking typewriter keys.

It was a stormy March night when "Aunty Flo" (I called her "Antiphlogistine" because she stuck so firmly) moved out. Quite by coincidence I was in the bathroom brushing my teeth when I heard her leaving. I've always been grateful that she let me know when she departed. There was no mistaking that prolonged furious rattling. Excitedly I grabbed a weapon — which turned out to be the icepick — as I ran through the kitchen, across the dining room and the long porch, and out around the house, still clutching the flashlight I'd been using for the toothbrush operation. When I saw Aunty Flo emerging from her retreat, and took in her huge size, I flew down the hill yelling for Delbert, who jumped into his pants and boots and came with the shotgun. The snake, of course, did not wait, but it was not difficult to track her as she wove her enormous curves through the tall weeds. We counted sixteen rattles.

The next fall my shelter for squatters was taken over by a family of skunks, which were harder to live with than the rattlesnake. They fought — whether with each other, or the rats and mice, or intruders of their own kind I never knew. But the weapon for offense or defense was the same one they aim at people who corner them. When chemical warfare started under the dining room, I had to leave my breakfast or supper and get out. When they fought at night, I had to take refuge in the car. The cottage was never free of the acrid unpleasantness of their fumes.

Poison was suggested, but I was ever against poison. Besides, if I had to have skunks, better have them alive than dead, under the floors. Finally Delbert and I came to terms about traps. I let him set one in my tenants' small entryway under the bathroom, provided a watch be kept so that no creature should suffer all night. A small chain, perhaps three feet long, fastened the trap to the standing waterpipe.

We did not have long to wait. When the rattling chain sounded the alarm, Delbert called his shaggy dog, Squeezix, who was afraid of nothing. I stood back with the flashlight; Delbert unwired the chain and gave it a fast jerking swing which landed the luckless skunk far out in the weeds where Squeezix killed it so fast it didn't know what struck it. Then Delbert reset the trap and went home, offering to come again on call.

I put on my warm flannelette pajamas, pumped up the gasoline lantern, and reached for my book, anticipating a pleasant hour or two on watch. Oh, oh! The chain rattled. I decided to be self-sufficient. Poor Delbert had worked hard and must be up at dawn to wrangle horses. Squeezix came at a gallop when I whistled. I didn't have to worry about his part of the operation.

I set the flashlight on the ground, unwound the wire, took a deep breath, straightened up, and gave the chain a mighty outward swing into space.

Squeezix got the skunk. But the skunk got me. Something was wrong with my swing technique. As she flew by, Mrs. Skunk gave me her final shot exactly amidships. However hard it was to take at the time, I gained firsthand knowledge about a legendary matter: you do not have to bury your clothes.

CHAPTER 15

Chicken

Halfway between the Homestead and the Windmill the Cowboy and I had made a nice round cement pila (drinking trough) ten feet in diameter and two feet deep to accommodate the cows in that locality so they would not have to walk another three miles to water. It was supplied by the pipeline coming down the canyon from the house well. Often when we pumped it ran over and wasted water. Later the Uncle, my schoolboy Trini, and I made a larger pila connected to the first and slightly lower to catch the overflow. We called this watering place *Dos Pilitas;* and I was pleased at seeing what a convenience and comfort it was to the wildlife. I made some smaller cement receptacles against the lower side for the quail and rabbits. When I stopped there to fill these little troughs with a bucket, I picked up a long lightweight stick (a dried sahuaro rib) and fished out the hundreds of bees drowning in the big pilas. I shoved the stick along the surface of the water until it was dark with halfdrowned bees, then — because they would never voluntarily let go — I tapped the stick against the four-inch wide top of the cement wall, leaving the bees to sit and get dry before flying away. When tired of standing I sat on the edge of the pila; if I put out my free hand to brace myself I was likely to get stung by an ingrate whose life I'd just saved. I tried putting sticks and boards in the water for rescue rafts, but they got waterlogged and were soon filled with dead bees.

I had no time or inclination to search for their hives (and the hunting neighbors had moved to the river) but that area seemed to be the center of a big bee settlement. In warm weather they came by the hundreds to drink there. There were thousands of them, crowding each other for a favorable place. As was bound to happen, many got dunked. Rarely did they have sense enough to turn back directly and grasp the rough concrete before getting their wings soaked. They scrambled around, got thoroughly wet, found nothing to cling to, and started swimming. They swam and swam, aimlessly, around and around, until they gave out and floated to death.

When I passed there, horseback or in the pickup, I stopped to check the water level, pour the small wildlife a drink, and found myself ending up as life-saver to bees. The men were right. It was a waste of time. But I couldn't help it. My conscience compelled me to stop and rescue the stupid bees. Maybe conscience isn't the right word. Perhaps inordinately imaginative people are super sensitive. There is a scornful name for the tendency to identify with creatures in distress: *chicken!* Okay. I'm it. I am that bee drowning lucklessly in deep water. Help!

Even more readily, I identify with larger creatures in jeopardy, and in proportionate degree.

There is no understanding Nature. Why are some of her creatures shy, attractive, loveable; and many downright curses to all other forms of life? And it is hard to figure out why man, since he is just as mortal and misery-plagued and pain-prone, has so little mercy on dumb animals. Laws have to be made and strictly enforced to restrain his brutish inclination to inflict suffering on creatures in his power.

These being my sentiments, I was the wrong rancher to contact for the purpose of borrowing, renting, or buying

at a bargain ten or fifteen head of calves to use in a local
rodeo. The young fellow came to me because small operators, being in perpetual need, are considered vulnerable.
Nobody would think of approaching a well-established
cattle ranch — say one that had been in the family for
generations and had cattle grazing on a thousand hills —
for such a deal as that.

With his own eyes the young man had evidence of my
financial difficulties, so he was quite taken aback when I
said firmly: "Over my dead body."

"It's a chance for all of us to make a little," he said.

"No," I said.

"You do sell calves, don't you?" he said aggressively.

"Not for rodeos."

"Don't you like rodeos?" He looked appalled.

"No. I like animals. No calf of mine will ever be
choused and mauled in the arena of a Roman circus."

"It don't hurt'm much," he argued, staring at me uncom-
prehendingly.

"How many legs have you broken?" I asked. "Or horns
knocked off?"

"We'll pay for 'm if they're hurt," he said.

"That won't help the animal any."

He frowned and shrugged and shook his head as he
turned to get into his car. He'd have to go clear to the
river to find other small cattle owners. The other ranches
in the vicinity were too big to listen to his proposition. He
and two other young men who were pretty good at roping
and riding, and didn't have money enough to hit the big-
time rodeos, had decided to promote a small show where
they could probably count on a dollar ticket from each
of the populace living in and around Oracle.

I don't know how much money they made, but they
did pull off the show.

Rodeos, which began under various names such as "stampedes," and "frontier days," are a class of entertainment which began on the American scene less than 100 years ago. A chief purpose of the rodeo is to make money. It remains a highly successful fund-raising operation throughout the circuit. As a rule, perhaps always, the sponsors — such as junior chambers of commerce — use the net proceeds for some worthy charity or city improvement. To make as much as possible, they organize their efforts, especially for publicity. Committees and group leaders work months in advance drumming up prizes and advertisements from the town merchants, selling tickets to all potential buyers, ballyhooing the great parade, selecting a queen, and lining up big name people — the governor, movie actresses, television personalities — to head the parade and give class to the opening (or parade) day of the show.

Sometimes in radio commercials I still hear the pitchmen saying that, in the rodeo, beholders will witness the cowboy skills used out on the range. Long ago that might have been true. Now there is very little open grazing land. The country is fenced; and cross-fenced into pastures. Ranchers have expensive corrals equipped with squeeze chutes and branding tables. They make their money from the weight on their cattle. They don't want them chased and thrown down, for it knocks off pounds. If they see a hired hand "busting" a calf it may be the worse for him.

But the American rodeo (banned in England and other European countries as cruelty to animals) has become a tradition. Like bullfighting in Spain and Mexico, it will be around, on the big circuit, for some time yet. In what is called now "the boondocks" and used to be spoken of as "out in the sticks," there is a change. Around every city and small town in Arizona, and probably all over the

West, there are men who keep horses for fun. They organize little roping clubs and frequently put on "ropings." They buy tough crossbred calves big enough to run. And if they kill or injure one it hurts them in the pocketbook.

A few years ago it was the custom on our river for ranchers to give rodeos to make a little needed cash, for livestock prices were very low. The owners and arena directors in charge got the county road equipment to bring in scrapers and bulldozers and clear a space. They put up barrier fences and holding pens and chutes, had tickets printed, barbecued a beef, cooked a tub of frijoles, and boiled gallons of coffee. A ticket entitled the holder to a plate of food at the end of the show. An outdoor activity, the show was held during hot weather. Loads of ice were required to cool the bottles of soda and cans of beer. Usually the turnout was good. It was a chance to visit with the neighbors, see the well-trained horses, and watch the local boys try their luck.

Some kind of music was furnished after the contests and the barbecue. Those young enough to ignore heat and dust could dance and romance. Baby-sitters and the old and middle-aged sat on benches or bales of hay and gossiped and watched others having more strenuous fun. It was a general good time and furnished a break in the lonely monotony of everyday work.

What about the cattle herded in and assaulted in the name of fun and a little jackpot money?

The last one I attended — the last I shall ever attend — used cows for the team tying. Cows! Mother cows! The rancher did not have any big steers with horns, so he gathered about a dozen cows for about three dozen cowboys to work on.

Out of the chute would trot a high-horned cow, worried at being cut away from her calf, scared out of her wits at all the noise and confusion of people and cars, having no idea in the world what was expected of her.

Down upon her would swoop a couple of ruthless horsemen frantically working their ropes against a stop watch. The cow picked up speed into a full gallop, her large udder swinging like a pendulum. The header jerked her to a halt with a tight loop over her horns. The heeler picked up her scrawny hind legs; they stretched her out in the dust and tied her down. It wasn't enough that she had done her part to carry on the ranch and the national economy. Now this indignity.

Was I the only spectator sickened by the sight?

Suddenly a skinny old *liviana* (speedy) cow picked up her heels and dashed over the soft ground to beat the horsemen to the safety line.

"Hooray!" I heard myself yelling. "Viva la vaca!"

A group of women around me (I had only just come to this area), probably most of them relatives of the rancher or the ropers, turned to stare at me hostilely. I hastily faded away.

And I have stayed away.

CHAPTER 16

That "Ole" Talk

Hearing sounds of horsebackers, I looked out of a back window one cold, blowy day to see the Old Cowman and the Chuck-Line Rider hitch their horses to the big mesquite in the yard and stamp across to the ramada where they took off their chaps and spurs. A moment later the Uncle greeted them at the door of the main cabin, and when they made straight to squat down by the open fire to warm their hands, he said, hospitably: "Will you fellers have off your coats?"

He threw another chunk of wood on the fire and was already raking out coals to heat the coffee and beans when he asked: "Have you all been to dinner?"

"We-ell," drawled the Rider, "Ain't airy one of us et no big sight today."

My ears perked up to catch the salty speech of the three old range men as they sat by the glowing fire happily warming themselves and joshing about the recent round-up — the Rider and the Cowman had taken part in it — of a dude neighbor they called Old Big Foot because he wore low-quartered shoes. Listening to their zesty vernacular as I went about warming the biscuits and setting the table, I knew it was the Past speaking. And I knew that soon, as history goes, all the current old-timers would be gone and I'd hear it no more. Nowadays, even cowboys attend school, respect dictionaries and grammars, and have their language standardized by mass communication media. I listened to the idioms and vocabularies of the old cronies with a regard almost tender because I knew their days were numbered, and that they spoke a vanishing tongue — each in his own way — for none of them could lay claim even to elementary schooling.

The Rider was a self-satisfied old fellow who had never in his life felt the need of formal instruction, particularly in self-expression — which he practiced continually. He loved to talk, and he never stopped as long as he could see that anybody was listening. He had to see his auditors, for he was so deaf it was hopeless to try to communicate with him unless you stood directly in front of him at close quarters and demanded his attention.

The Old Cowman had made it through the fourth reader before he ceased being classified as a child, and from that day forward, he never read another book. In fact he did not read anything except a few headlines and the livestock reports. At the age of nine, big for his years, he joined the wranglers in charge of a remuda. From there his rank progressed to rider, *jinete* (bronc buster), cowboy, and — finally out for himself — cowman.

The Uncle's book learning ended abruptly in the lower grades back in the eighties when a teacher slapped him. Seven years later he slapped her back. In that day Texans, whatever their speech, proudly held their bodies inviolate. They had elephant memories for insults and injuries; their wide shoulders were seldom chipless. In that day and on into the present century's first decades, no man in the state of Texas called another a liar or s.o.b. unless ready for mortal combat.

The hand of Time moving down the ages has tempered the passions of outlaws and frontiersmen. Public education has smoothed the tongues of rugged individuals with a gloss of common usage — including the general use of profanity by men, women, and children. There is a sameness about American speech today. Sometimes out here in the back country there are exceptions. Curley had worked on ranches here and there during most of his adolescence. He hadn't done well in school so his father farmed him out to cattlemen. He came to the GF Bar several times between jobs. In the presence of a schoolteacher he made an effort with his English which greatly amused the nephews.

At breakfast he told them that he had just met me by *co-accident* at the gas station. The night before, as we drove home, when we got to the top of McKinsey Hill — the long curving descent into the canyon — a little calf jumped into the road ahead and galloped along the narrow cut in front of the car, making it hard to drive. I put on the dim lights, blew the horn, beat on the outside of the door, and crept along for awhile with the parking lights only. Nothing worked. The mischievous little rascal wouldn't get out of the way.

"What an aggravation!" I said.

"Yes, ma'am," said Curley, "it's plumb disencouraging."

He told us that he didn't want a job in the mine because his oldest brother had worked in mines and got *sili-kitis*. He didn't care much for his last boss, but he was a *jokable feller*, you could say that.

In the old days, adventuring men and women of the great wild West practically handcarved their speech just as they hewed their furniture and whittled their accessories. In limited cultural environment there was little need for erudite vocabularies. Today, even in the Far West, people are alert and striving to be up to date in everything, including oral expression. Nobody disapproves of that. It is a good thing for American youth to learn correct

English; in fact, it is essential. Nevertheless, and with due respect and apologies, there is a nostalgic attraction about "that old talk" of our predecessors.

In listing surviving provincialism of the western "horse" areas, the word found most frequently — with no literal meaning in the dictionary sense — is *old,* pronounced *ole.* The Uncle had to feed his ole dogs, saddle his ole pony, "ile" his ole gun, find his ole hat.

"That ole snip-nosed sorrel" had nothing to do with the horse's age.

"That ole brockly-faced steer" might be only a two-year-old.

The boss was always The Ole Man, even if only nineteen years old. Here it was that I posed a problem. I have been the boss of this outfit almost since the beginning, but obviously of the wrong sex. "Ole Woman" is downgrading. So in my case, the men on the place, when wanting to be formal, have resorted to Spanish — calling me *La Patrona* or *La Maestra.* Ordinarily they have addressed me by the name I've always been called: Sister. (Ole Sister?)

Associates, favored or despised, always had *ole* preceding their names. Ole Johnny was just a kid. Ole Mike was a popular bronc rider. Ole Hawkins was a disliked neighbor. Ole Hoover was ex-President of the United States.

I remember sitting around the fire eating late dinner at a roundup, when a dude was seen approaching, jogging along on a head-slinging pony. All stared, sizing up the situation, and someone muttered: "Here comes Ole Ignorance."

Ole Big Mouth was a garrulous homesteader generally shunned because he was so windy. Ole Pussyfoot was a newcomer who strained openly to stand in with the boss.

Ole Broadie was a middle-aged woman who took up a homestead on the open range grazed by cattle from three different outfits.

One of the Valley cowboys got married, and his thoughtless town bride followed him about to all the accessible camps on the work. One morning when "passeling" out mounts for each man's string, the roundup foreman said: "Give that little ole jug-headed Diamond-A bay to Ole Honey."

Ole Bumblefoot was a fellow prone to accidents and mistakes. Ole Bolliver may never have known how he got his range moniker, but everybody else knew. They were bringing a herd to a working corral in a lonely flat up on the divide when up rode a town guy — he "follered" the plumber's trade — who had recently filed on a section of grazing land in the vicinity. Greenhorn that he was, he sat his horse near an open gate and watched the wild cattle whirl and mill and give the cowpunchers a bad time. Exasperated, the Old Cowman, who had never set eyes on him before, rode over and hollered: "Bolliver, will you get your car-kass out of that gate so we can pen these cattle!" From then on, even after he won his spurs with the cowboys, he was always Bolliver.

Probably the word *man* rates second place in cowboyese. One use is as an expletive. "Man-oh-man! Ain't this a scorcher!" "Man alive! I like to a-froze to death last night."

Commonly it was — and is yet — used to express in third person, an idea referring to the first person singular. "A man cain't do only so much." "If a man could count on it a-rainin'." "Looks like a man got to sell his ole pore cows." "A man jest nachally orter light in an' buffalo them plow-chasin' homesteaders as fast as they show up."

Food, to the old range boys, was chuck, grub, or vittles. The Uncle made excellent biscuits which he called "bread."

The wrapped loaves I brought from town were "light bread." He made a good stew he called "mulligan." And a rice - and - raisins - and - lots - of - sugar dessert which was "moonshine." He boiled sugar and water to make "lick." Bought syrup, no matter what kind, was "lasses." When I asked him if he liked something I had made or bought that he had not eaten before, he'd say: "I reckin it's tol'able good."

Two life-supporting staples contributed to the West by Mexico have survived almost unchanged for more than two centuries: frijoles (dried pink or pinto beans), and jerky — a corruption of the South American *charque* (sun-dried meat).

There's something frustrating about cowpunching and horse breaking that riles a man's ire. If he couldn't cuss he'd blow up. Many are the range expressions describing aggravation or fury. Range riders say:

"The old man's on the prod."
"Cookie is ringie this mornin'."
"The old lady got wrathy about the mud on her floor."
"The boss has been swelled up for a week."

There were some ranchers — son and brother of a cow-man whose womenfolks lived in town — who often complained that the old man worked them like slaves and didn't know the difference between day and night when it came to getting a job done. The brother was supposed to work for hire, and that put a crimp in his resentment, when he felt he'd been mistreated. The son worked for the ranch's sake and for duty's sake and for the hope of one day having something of his own. As the years passed and he grew into manhood, the boss became ever more decrepit. He became so stove-up he could no longer work horseback. His gaunt frame looked like a walking defunct.

Still, he ran the outfit, mostly "by jawbone," haranguing the men nights when they rode in, and mornings before they rode out. To the brother's satisfaction, the son began to talk back. One evening the grumbling old man said, "Hard work never hurt nobody."

"How do you know?" asked the defiant son.

"I know by my own self," declared the boss hotly. "I worked hard all my life."

"And jist look at you," retorted the son. "Y'ought to go out and advertise. Show y'self as an example, and there wouldn't nary son-of-a-bitch ever work again!"

The brother was one of the most colorful characters the West produced — at least in this century. One day he told me his philosophy. "Sister," he said earnestly, "I ain't honest, but I'm honorable. I don't steal from women."

If you are a schoolteacher, you almost have to nip in the bud all deviations from the accepted norm in the speech of the young entrusted to your influence. And if you were an English major, shame on you for treasonable fondness for what must be classed incorrect, uncouth, archaic. Forgive me, highly esteemed English professors who labored to instruct me in the elegancies and modernities of the world's most varied language. I do enjoy "that ole talk." I'll be sorry when the scattered few who speak it unaffectedly are with us no more.

CHAPTER 17

And More Cows

I remember the exact moment when I lost my heart to bovines. I was following the Old Cowman along a lonely trail in and out of deep canyons, my whole attention focused on trying to keep up with his horse's expert pace without the disgrace of letting my pony break into a trot. Going down a brushy ridge, all at once he stopped beside a thickly spreading bush, got off, and parted the branches.

"Want to see somethin' purty?"

I rode up to see something pretty, surprised at his interest.

"Oh!" I exclaimed in quick delight, looking down into the uplifted face of a new baby calf curled up cozily beneath the leafy branches. He returned my gaze with the wide eyes of innocence and unflawed beauty. His mother had washed him clean and dry and left him hidden in what seemed to her a safe spot while she went for water. His nose and inner ears were pink. His small face was snowy white, with a baby softness, and so was the line down his back. According to the standards of that day, the line would detract from his value as a steer, but now all that white contrasted with the shine of his red coat to give him extra charm. He was lovely, and I loved him. And he was mine; the first new calf born to the little bunch of cows I had bought a few months before.

Many years have passed, but I still love baby calves

and thrill to see each new arrival. Of course, all baby creatures have the attraction of miniature replicas. But little calves are special. With their pink noses, curly faces, big ears, and luminous trusting eyes, they are among the cutest baby creatures on earth. I often wonder how such dear little things can grow up into big old rough — often repulsive-looking — cows and bulls. But then, I wonder in the same vein about human infants.

Modern publications devoted to the interests of ranchers often print articles whose intent is to standardize the operation of cattle growing.

"We are in the beef business," said an authority. "We are not raising individuals."

That idea can be challenged.

Cattle are live creatures, procreating and nourishing their young by their own bodies. Like all mammals, including mankind, they live and die as individuals. As all mammals do, they come into the world through the same dark pain-ridden tunnel; they leave it through the same door of death. They encounter earthly pleasures, joys, hazards, and torments from the moment of conception, even as we do. And like us, they meet those mundane trials as single identities and develop idiosyncrasies, each in a special way, from the day they are born.

The old trail-driving cowboys, who punched the herds of longhorns up the long, winding trails to Kansas and Wyoming and Montana in the early years of the American cattle industry, found that to be true. In day-by-day association, they learned that their critters not only did not look alike, they did not act alike. Some were handsomely gifted in coloring and conformation; others were ugly as "h'ants." Some were leaders, naturally taking charge of certain groups, large or small; breaking trail for them, setting the pace, seeking likely places for them to graze.

Others were loners shunning the crowds, incessantly planning to make a getaway, taking every chance to dash for freedom. There were Fiery and Snuffy, easily spooked, always looking for a chance to stampede the masses. There were man hating *mañosos,* and incorrigible ranahans who would never yield and "throw up their tails." Also, there were placid, good-natured ones seeking to conform and keep the peace, usually too lazy to do anything but poke along with the drags. Some were easy keepers, fattening on the sketchy grazing they could pick up on the go; others "et so much it kep'm pore to pack it along." All were individuals.

No matter how much a ranch may be modernized and mechanized, cattle, as long as they live, can never be merely the end products of mass production. Scientific feeding and selection and artificial insemination and automatic handling methods, yes; but in the most up-to-date livestock enterprise that can be found in a materialistic profit-making industry, it still takes a cow nine months to bring forth a calf, and another nine months or so to nourish him properly from her own flesh and blood.

Many people inexperienced in close association with bovines have the idea that producing the young comes easily and painlessly to a cow because "Nature takes care of everything." Not so. A great many cows, perhaps the majority, meet their delivery time as insecurely as women. I have no statistics, and must speak from experience and observation. My conclusion is that a surprising number of cows have serious trouble giving birth, especially young heifers with first calves. Many of them "sluff" their young before they are fully matured, and usually these "preemies" die. There are no incubators for them. You wrap them in gunny sacks and pour warm milk down them, but you can't save them.

Even grown cows, some quite experienced, endure hazardous suffering in their travail. And at times they, too, must die.

Two boys hunting up in the high country came upon a starving baby calf standing forlornly by his lifeless mother. In his extremity he tried to follow them after they had stopped to pet him. They couldn't leave him. They carried him down to their Jeep and brought him to me. It wasn't easy to save him. Making up a formula and getting the right amount at the right time down newborn calves that have not had their mother's first milk, is chancy. With the best intentions, you can kill them. There was the question, too, about my right to him. I went to the owner of the cattle in the area where the boys were hunting and explained the dilemma of the orphan calf.

"Keep the thing," he said at once, "if you can raise it. I haven't got time to fool with a dogie."

I named the little bull Jerry-Fred, for his rescuers. When a few weeks had passed, I could entertain guests by walking into the corral with a big pop bottle of warm milk and letting them watch Jerry-Fred's antics. He would come at a gallop and latch onto the bottle, gulping noisily. When it was empty he would chase me across the corral, begging for more.

The same neighbor, while working his river cattle, found another dogie and brought him up to me. He was part Brahma, light in color, and so bony we called him *Huilo* (wé-lo, meaning skinny). He soon developed so much strength, and skill with the bottle, that he could knock me off balance. I put him in the small calf pen and fed him through the bars of the gate. Sometimes I put both dogies in the little enclosure and stuck two bottles of milk through the fence. Huilo quickly chug-a-lugged his and pushed Jerry-Fred aside to get his also.

Effie Jo, one of the pet cows I have now, was orphaned at birth. I went down to start the pump one day and stopped at the feed trough to put out booster cubes for the cows that water at the spring. I was shocked to see this midget — nothing but skin and bones — trying to get a sup of milk from every cow around her. When one pushed her off, she turned to try the next. Cows are gentle with these helpless babies. They don't want to hurt them, although as a rule, they won't let them have any milk. To get rid of them they raise a hind leg and shove the strange baby away. If shoving with a leg isn't enough, they nudge the little intruder away with lowered heads. Even wild cows are gentle with motherless little calves.

When I got the pump going I picked up the starved foundling, who was still persisting in trying to do what came naturally, and put her in the Jeep beside me to take her to the home corral. At first I started her on canned milk with a beaten egg, then for awhile graduated her to a fresh cow that gave more milk than her calf could take. When another cow giving more milk "came in" I again changed her foster mother. As she grew huskier and nudged harder, no cow would put up with her. I had to tie the cow to a snubbing post and bind her hind legs with a short rope to make her safe to approach. This was the healthiest dogie I ever tried to raise. Her sides would stick out like a balloon, but she would hang on for the last drop. No matter how much she overate — that spring there were several cows with surplus milk — she never "scoured." In fact, she has never had a sick day in her life. No matter how many cows needed milking out, as soon as one was tied up she was Nellie-on-the-Spot. Neighbor Pete called her the Milking Machine. Johnny, a small great-nephew visiting his grandmother (my sister Ruby) at the ranch was fascinated by this ravenous young dogie.

"What do you think we ought to name her?" I asked.
"Heifer Jo," he answered immediately.

That evolved into Effie Jo. Even when she was three years old and had a calf of her own, we dared not tie up a cow with a big bag while Effie was in the corral.

The day I found her, I went hunting for her mother and discovered her corpse up the canyon in a brushy place she had selected for her delivery room.

It is not unusual for a cow out on the range to die at giving birth. It happens on everybody's ranch. It is unusual for the little calf to live. If he doesn't freeze or starve to death, the varmints get him. Most of the time, cows die before the calf is delivered, so both are lost. Many of the young heifers I keep for replacements calve too young because my range is too small to offer them escape from early motherhood. They often have trouble. When I see one of the poor things "making a bag" I shut her up in the hospital corral and feed her alfalfa (for vitamin A) and watch her. Sometimes she must have human assistance.

Little Ice Cream was a case in point. That was during the Nephew's tenancy. He came to my door early one morning saying: "Ice Cream is down and about to die. The calf is only half-born, and it's already dead."

I got a move on, and we tried pulling it by hand. We couldn't. I saddled my pony and tied a rope to the little front feet, but that didn't work. The young cow was too near dead to help. As a last resort we put a rope around her chest and anchored it to the corral fence, then fastened another rope to the little forefeet and pulled the dead calf with the Jeep.

There was a cow's scream of terror and pain, and Ice Cream lay gasping for life. All we knew to do for her, was to wait and hope and offer her a few bottles of water. The dead calf was a beautiful bull, too well-developed for easy entrance through life's portal. In a little while, the heifer was sufficiently recovered to stagger to her feet and drink water from a bucket. She got well and has had no trouble with subsequent calves although the vet was shocked at what we had done. He explained in anatomical terms why such drastic measures would ruin the cow. However, by the therapy of ignorance, we saved her life.

The latest horror story in this line has to do with a nice young cow we call Redington, fully matured, who had already mothered two good calves. It was during the cholla-burning, so a week or two before her time I shut her up in the hospital corral and fed her hay. The Nephew had gone away to college. Jesús, my immigrant friend, was in tenure as cowboy. One busy morning he came to tell me that Redington was having her calf.

"She'll be all right," I said, and an hour later went down to greet the new arrival.

It was still unborn. The cow was in real distress; walking and walking, then lying down, then getting up, all the time in labor. Only one little foot was exposed. Why should this be? I didn't know what to do. After another hour (the cow in the same condition and growing weaker), Neighbor Pete came down and the three of us decided to take the calf "by instruments" (ropes and human strength).

The exhausted cow, in extreme anguish, made no resistance, but we went through the motions of tying her to a post. I rolled up my sleeves, soaped my hands and arms, and went for that other front foot. It was doubled back. I could get hold of it all right, but found that the head was doubled back also, so that the shoulder was presented and birth was impossible. The men insisted on trying. But why prolong the torture? I backed the pickup to the chute, we practically carried her up into it, and I started a rush journey over the rough road to the vet — sixty miles away.

For years I had been a patron of this animal doctor, one of the first, as far as I knew, to practice, with proper credentials, in this area. Many times he had gone beyond the call of ordinary duty for my suffering creatures. Now he had come to have a reputation for alcoholism. When I mentioned him, friends and neighbors shook their heads.

"But he's a *doctor*," I insisted, "a born doctor, and trained. He has what it takes."

Redington's case was proof of this. It was a terrible trip — the poor cow struggling to keep upright, I anxiously looking back, doing my best to make time. I had to go through a congested fringe of the city and pass a large school at fifteen miles an hour. Although most of the children were indoors, a few were scattered about outside. I regretted the shock it might give them to see a cow with a protruding calf's foreleg dangling.

It had been months since I had contacted the doctor. His wife told me that he had given up working on large animals. I insisted on seeing him.

"He'll have to help me!" I stated.

He came out, took a look at the cow, and told me to back up to the ramp. His eyes looked like the proverbial burnt holes in a blanket. It was apparent he had been ill. His hands trembled when he helped me open the rack and tie Redington's head to the front of it. But I was relieved. I had faith in him as a talented doctor with the nerve to try, and a gift for healing. I watched in admiration. There was no fumbling and experimenting. He knew what he was doing and wasted no time or words. His shirt was thrown aside. He lathered his hands and arms with the disinfectant suds in the large pan I held for him, and went in to put the fouled-up calf into its proper channel. The moaning cow got lower and lower, but her feet were wide apart, and he held her up with his shoulder, struggling to keep from falling himself. Twice he had to stop and get his breath, like a mountain climber who goes too fast. Suddenly he sat down. My heart sank. Had he quit? No. He looked up at me proudly and gasped: "I've got the nose out."

Sure enough, there was a little nose — ominously purple — resting on *two* front feet.

"It's dead," I said.

"It's *not* dead," he scolded, getting up. "Here, pull on this chain when I tell you to."

I pulled with all my might while he used his hands as instruments.

Out came the calf.

The cow screamed and fell to the floor of the truck, unable to get up or even move during the two-hour journey home. We put the wet, shaking calf up by her head for encouragement. She was too sick to care. I covered it with a gunny sack and drove as fast as I dared, not taking time to thank the doctor or ask his fee. (It was $6.00.)

Even when I backed up to her own corral and let the endgate down, Redington couldn't get up. Jesús helped me put a pile of hay and gunny sacks at the foot of the truck, and we yanked and tumbled her out and laid the calf by her side, hoping Nature would take over at last. Nature did. When Jesús brought Redington a bucket of water she sat up and drank eagerly, then began lowing to her calf and nuzzling it. I threw my hat in the air with joy. Next day mother and daughter were doing fine. We call the heifer *Milagro* (Miracle).

Bernice (my youngest sister) grew up in town. She does not have the feeling for country things that I have. But visiting the ranch one Christmas, down at the corral she broke into ecstasies when she saw a baby calf peeking at her through the bars.

"Look!" she cried. "Look at its big eyes and long eyelashes! It looks just like a Disney drawing. I know where he gets his models now. Do call this one Disney."

So we named the wee heifer Disney (soon corrupted to Dizzy) Riley, Riley being her family name.

When I came into control of a homestead and some leased land and hesitantly fell into the cattle business, the first bunch I bought contained fifty cows. One was solid brown, so she was Old Brownie. One had white stripes arranged on her back and shoulders in such a way that she became Old Dog Harness. Forty-eight were left to be named. What more natural than to call them after the states? These were so named, and they became the progenitors of the First Families of the GF Bar. The Cowboy took up with the idea at once. When he left, the Uncle finally caught on to the logic of it. I explained that it was simpler to say "Old Iowa" than "that old gauch-horned white-faced cow that waters at Dos Pilitas." He agreed, with reservations.

"If I kin jist recollect their flesh marks," he complained. It was hard for him to remember what each cow looked like.

The Old Vaquero, when he arrived on the scene, had trouble of a different kind. He knew cattle! When he laid eyes on a cow he could recognize her from then on. "I wish," he used to say (in Spanish, of course) "that I could know people as well as I do cows."

But there were very few of the forty-eight states he had ever heard of. And as a rule their pronunciation threw him. To tell the truth, I enjoyed his individual way of designating the GF Bar cows. He used a double name for them: *la cabrona Nuevo Yorqui, la cabrona Nuevo Mejico, la cabrona Persivania, la cabrona Qui Anza* (Kansas), *la cabrona Masa Chusey.* His favorite name was Ok-la-ho-ma, and he always insisted on having one by that name when we sold the original.

When I bought the hundred Mexico cows, we were hard-pressed to find — all at once — enough names for them to enter on the ranch register. The Old Vaquero christened many of them: Concha, Comadre, Sonza, Cola Negra, Cucaracha, always putting his prefix to each moniker.

When the Uncle spoke of "that old high-horned bald-faced pale-red cow from the Tank that's wild as a snake," I said, "Why not call her Old Snake?" She became Old Rattlesnake and put the fear of death into anyone who came near when she had a baby calf.

My bulls are named for persons: sometimes the original owner, such as Old Harrison; or the speculator I bought him from, Rocky Solano; or the boys on the ranch at the time of purchase: Victor, Arturo, Rocky Donn. My best bull is named Felix — for my banker.

When I got the crossbred cows (fathered by Brahma bulls out of white-faced cows) I gave them Latin-American names. For a while we had most of South and Central America and some of the West Indies. We still have Chile, Argentina, Bolivia, Brazilia, Santiago, Santo Domingo, and Buenos Aires.

Peru, by her behavior characteristics, came to be called Old "Brayma" Lion. She is a cow from Bitter Creek, right up at the Headwaters. We have more fun and more work with her than with any other cow ever on the ranch. She looks like a gargoyle; huge and square of stature, dark maroon-red except her face, which is dotted with freckles. Around her eyes are two oval dark spots edged with what looks like white lace. Her horns are turned grotesquely, one pointing up and one turned inward over her forehead, and her udder has long since sagged from overweight. Her behavior is actively unfriendly although she accepts me — and, for the time being, Neighbor Pete — as being tolerable as long as alfalfa and dairy feed are doled out to her when she has a little calf. We must never, however, let our guards down.

She holds an unmitigated grudge against strangers, particularly those wearing skirts. When a visitor appears around the corrals, even when Old Brayma is calfless and free, she hoists her head like an alerted stallion, then lowers it menacingly, steps forward with a baleful look, and slowly paws the ground with first one huge forefoot, then the other. It never fails to ensure her privacy.

She can roar in fine imitation of a wild African lion — hence her name — with little follow-up rumbles. And when she has a new calf she is as dangerous as I imagine an aroused lion to be. She never tames down, even when I have kept her, apparently docile, in the delivery corral eating alfalfa for a week or two before the calf is born. As soon as it arrives she is on the fight.

The first few days not even her keeper (me) is allowed in the corral with Old Brayma and her offspring. She has no conscience about putting up with the hand that feeds her. I throw a little hay close to the dividing fence, then reach over to get a stout rope around her head and anchor her to a fence post. After that I can enter, keeping my distance so she can't reach me with her head, tie up her hind legs, then get the baby and push him into place and teach him to eat naturally. It is a task requiring several days during which I have to milk the cow and feed him via a pop bottle. While I'm trying to help him, his mother, pretending to be absorbed in food but watching her chance, makes sudden jerks and thrusts and sometimes bumps me. Once she swung at Neighbor Pete and, unable to reach him with her head, swiped the glasses from his face with her long rough tongue.

One year I didn't find her in time and she developed mastitis so severely that one chamber went into gangrene and was lost. Old Brayma was so near death I almost despaired of saving her. It seemed hopeless, but I worked on in despair even when she was down. Shots of penicillin for eleven consecutive days, and daily local treatments with antibiotic tubes were not enough. I decided to treat her as if she were human and apply ice-packs. The medication had put her on her feet, but the chamber was swollen and turning black. The ice remedy was not easy to administer. I kept the snubbing post between her and me until I got the rope flipped over her head. As soon as she was caught she let me lead her close enough to tie her to the post. Even when tied, to uphold her honor she sometimes made snorty rushes at me, not really meaning anything serious. As soon as I hobbled her hind legs and tied down her lashing tail, she was in my hands. I made a very complicated harness of wide strips of gunny sacking to which I tied a thick cotton bag filled with chipped ice and covered with a doubled burlap bag to keep it clean and retain the cold longer. Every hour, I went down with more ice, or, when she was better, ice water to cool the bandage.

When it became necessary for me to make a trip to the city, Hoppy, one of the summer nephews, took over the ice-water routine. He had a story to tell when I returned. Alone at the ranch, he decided to get an over-all sun tan. When he appeared in the corral wearing only shoes and a man's bikini, Old Brayma put him out in a hurry. He returned to the house and put on a shirt and Levi's. Still he was refused admittance. On the third try he donned one of my old straw hats, and was able to pass inspection and go ahead with the treatment. Since that time, I have done a better job of watching her and she is healthy enough, although her surplus milk makes it necessary to pen her twice a day for milking until her calf is at least two or three months old.

Why don't I sell her? Sad will be the day when I shall have to. I admire her spirit and her ability to keep fat, good times or bad. She has a nice calf every year. Cub, her last, weighed 510 pounds when sold at the age of ten months. She always puts on a good show. That roar! Good old Brayma Lion. Time cannot change or custom stale her infinite variety.

There's heartbreak in caring for animals. Their lives are so short and it hurts to see them go. I was sick to tears the last time I took a cow to the auction pens. It was Old Pepper Sauce, long a pillar of the *ranchito*. Time came to save her heifer and sell her. She was never a wild cow, but she fought every inch of the way and broke the loading chute as the Neighbor and I shoved her into the truck. I had placed some good hay up front for her to nibble on while I changed clothes, and while I hunted for the inspector. She wouldn't touch it. She rode backwards, looking homeward all the way.

When Carlos and I unloaded her at the sales corrals and pushed her down the chute into the holding area — rather a large space — she turned and raised her head and stared at me as I closed the chute gates and made the truck ready to leave. I cannot forget that look. It brought tears. She was saying: *"You* can do this to me?"

With the exception of neurotics and outlaws, animals are easy to love. The better you know them, the more you cherish them. The cows I am more closely associated with are the milk cows that live near the corrals, so they are my favorites.

Our first at the homestead was a very old off-white Jersey

of giant size. She was from a farm down on the river, and
the Cowboy traded a horse and a range cow for her and
brought her home through the cholla patches as a Christmas surprise. The chollas were a terrible surprise to *her,*
and she arrived as full of stickers as a porcupine. We picked
them out and fed her well and named her Vanilla. It
wasn't long until she brought forth a big heifer calf —
sired by a Hereford bull — dark seal-brown in color with
a white face. We called her Chocolate. Old Vanilla gave
so much milk we put a little red dogie on her. It became
Strawberry. The owners had only parted with Vanilla
because of her advanced age, and that was the reason we
sold her when the calves were big enough to wean. We
intended Chocolate to succeed her as ranch milk cow, but
she didn't qualify and got turned out on the range. After
several bull calves, she produced a heifer dull yellow in
color — the neighbors had a fence-jumping half-Brahma
bull — which we named Butterscotch. *Her* first heifer was
named Vanilla. She has a string of daughters still here
on the ranch: Pudding, Milk Shake, Ice Cream, all noted
for having bull calves.

Our second milk cow was a beautiful little pure Guern-
sey that my sister Ruby gave us from her small dairy farm
near Mesa. She was only a few days old when we brought
her home in the back seat of the sedan. She had a white
heart in the middle of her forehead so perfect it might have
been a paper cutout, so we called her Sweetheart. She was
a great help and comfort to us. When she graduated into
production the Uncle took her over as his special pet. One
day he gave her a big feed of first-cutting alfalfa and rode
off to inspect the lower fence. When he returned several
hours later, he found Sweetheart stretched out dead from
bloat. (With money scarcer than hen's teeth, I had paid
for a bale of hay that killed our precious cow.) Coming

home from school Friday evening, I passed a great excavation and mound of sand in the canyon bottom where the broken-hearted Uncle had tried to bury her as a member of the family. And like a member of the family, she left us a legacy: her nice little dark-colored, white-faced heifer Dolly, who eventually became the milk cow and reigned as queen of the ranch for many a day.

Finally I was confronted with the awful problem posed by all beloved pets: what to do with Dolly as she steadily grew too old to continue in the life we shared.

Science books (for school children) give the life span of a cow as twenty years. But that, surely, relates to some bovine Methuselah. Buyers call a cow old at eight. Certainly after ten they are in their "golden years."

What would the ranch be without good, faithful Dolly? But I could not see her suffer starvation when her teeth gave out. When she was thirteen, I weaned myself from her by taking her and her pretty bull calf to a nice green permanent pasture twenty miles down the river, with three other good old cows who had been her pals and my mortgage-lifters. After five months I had got used to the ranch without Dolly. She was fat as a butter ball, and so was her calf. I let her and her fat cronies be taken to the sale in the city. She weighed only twenty pounds under a thousand, according to the slips sent with the check. I could not bear to be present when she was sold.

It is a characteristic of milk cows to have bull calves. Dolly's were husky, mischievous corral inhabitants that the Uncle invariably called Meanness for their sassy habits of pushing past him into the hay barn, sticking their noses into his milk pail, or chewing up his saddle straps when they got a chance. By a real stroke of luck Dolly finally had a heifer — her next-to-last calf. It wasn't long until my delight turned to dismay, for the sorry-looking little scrawny female didn't make a worthy stand-in for her mother. She was brindle — a non-pretty color — on her hips. She was red-necked, narrow-headed, spindle-legged, bony-hipped, and her eyes streamed water. Her nose, wet from mother's milk, was streaked with dust. We called her Dirty Face, and I fully intended to sell her when she got to be a yearling.

But that was the year of the Big Move to a rougher canyon. Rains were scarce. Feed was short. Poor little Dirty Face was too skinny to sell. There was good grass over here, so we turned her loose and forgot about her. Months later she showed up as a long-yearling; she was nice and fat, but extremely pregnant. We were stuck with her. And that, my cynical colleagues, was my biggest blessing in disguise.

Dirty Face is now my favorite favorite-cow. She has been worth her weight in so many things. How could I get along without her?

She won my sympathy and esteem when, too young to be a mother, she had her first calf, a big, fully-developed bull, and became my first subject in the practice of midwifery. It was a snowy day of low clouds and cold wind when the poor little heifer arrived at her time, thereby initiating me into a new catalogue of troubles but winning my heart in doing so. I was keeping her up and feeding her. Couldn't Nature handle the rest of the miserable job? It seemed logical to think so, but my uneasiness increased as the hours of labor dragged on. Was she going to die right before my helpless eyes?

Taking on the duties of obstetrician was something I didn't want. Why, I mused in bitterness, was Nature fool enough to start something she couldn't finish. Didn't she alone instigate the whole unsanitary, often disgusting, altogether undignified, apparently unsafe method of carrying on the species? Now it was up to me, an ignoramus with not even a What-To-Do Book, to improve on the situation, and save some lives. I kept watching and hoping until dark. To protect the tormented heifer and impending new life from the cold wind and spitting snow, I shut her up in the barn. By my warm fire, tempering anxiety with an interesting book, I waited — going down every half hour to check on how Dirty Face was doing. She wasn't doing any good.

When the futile labor had been going on for at least six hours, I lost hope. The Uncle, pushing eighty years, had gone to bed. I went in to wake him and tell him I was going across the Valley to Wallace, a former neighbor, and ask him to come help me.

"She is down broadside," I told him. "She can't have that calf."

"Sister," remonstrated the Uncle, "we can pull that calf. She'd be dead anyway time you got back."

He dressed and fired up his old kerosene lantern, picked up his walking stick, and went down to boss the job I dreaded and feared.

Dirty Face had kept sliding downhill until she was in a huddle by the door. We dragged her back into a cleared area, and I eagerly followed the Uncle's directions. When all was ready he stood at the head and pulled her tail while I, at her feet, pulled the rope. Eureka! There entered into this life another big fat "Meanness."

The little cow — as soon as a heifer has a calf she is counted a cow, even if she is no bigger than a peanut — got right up and began the silliest, happiest taking-on, lowing and mumbling, tickled to death over her first-born. We laughed at the ridiculous fuss she made over the messy little bull, licking him, practically singing him a lullaby, not trying to look out for herself although she trembled from weakness so that she could hardly stand.

"She thinks that's the only calf in the world," remarked the Uncle, as proud of the mother and baby as I was.

What a good little cow she was! What a good little cow she has been ever since — never losing that rapturous joy in motherhood although she has had more calves than any cow ever branded GF Bar.

She and I have a comedy routine that gives us both satisfaction. I come out into the early morning sunshine, headed for the corrals. As I walk along the path I stop to gaze toward the east where she ranges, and cry: "DIRRRRRTY FAAACE!"

From across two deep, rough-sided gullies comes the answer:

"WHAAAAAAUT-TTT?"

"You come on over here, that's what."

She is nowhere in sight. I call sharply: "YOU DIRTY FACE!"

"YAHHHHHHHHUH."

I shade my eyes with my hand and see her emerge from behind a palo verde she has been nibbling on. "Come on, now. You hurry up."

She answers that she is coming directly, and in a few seconds she has stumbled over the rocks and around the cactus and is on the road. By the time I have fed the horses and put her rations into the manger, she is at the gate.

This little matutinal performance makes me glad. It helps to compensate for womanly joys and properties that I have missed, and the physical comforts I renounced when I took to the canyons. It lifts my vanity. I don't know anyone else who goes out in the morning and calls in a cow from the wide-open spaces. It's an archaic custom from two or three centuries back. There was the English poet who sang "Co-Boss, Co-Boss" till the cows came home.

In that day cows played an intimate and vital part in family life. Those I know who still milk their own usually have bells on their "bossies," and go out in the dawn to listen to the tinkling as they drive the laggards in. Only my Dirty Face answers when paged.

Although she answers only me, she knows her name any time. There may be several cows penned-up for feeding or doctoring. When I open the outside gate and call: "Dirty Face, you go out. Dirty Face!" she gives up licking her empty feed trough and marches out with queenly aplomb. In this respect she will heed anyone she knows — the Nephew, the Neighbor, even Jesús who says: "Dooty Fes."

She is not pretty, not well-bred. She looks like a little old *corriente*. But beauty isn't everything. She gives a gallon of milk from one chamber twice a day, leaving three gallons for her calf and whatever dogie may be in need. Her prime qualification is that she is, as we say on the range, a calf-haver. In ten years she has presented the outfit with twelve calves. If she has a calf in February, she's likely to have another in December of the same year. One year she had three calves: twins born in March, and another little bull in December, all of them good. She gets the production medal on my place.

Twins are rare among bovines. Dirty Face is the only cow I have owned that has had them. And I learned something because the twins were male and female. The heifer was the first Dirty Face had had, so I naturally planned to keep it to take her place some day. But when the twins were almost a year old, I read in a novel (the setting of which was a farm in Vermont) that in the case of twins of opposite sexes, the heifer would be barren. This was confirmed by the state veterinarian. It didn't seem logical and I kept hoping. But when the heifer was two years old the truth was obvious. She had no sign of feminine curves and her fat was not the soft plumpness of the mother type, but the solid weight of a barren cow. Sadly I brushed her off and sent the Nephew to take her as a donation to the crippled children's hospital in Tucson, where it was our turn to contribute a beef. Subsequently I had a letter from the director thanking me, saying that the packer who butchered the heifer appraised her as being worth $150.

Strange to say, Dirty Face's last calves have been heifers. Now that she is heading down the last mile, I worry, and watch constantly for signs of cancer-eye or toothlessness — some dreaded infirmity that will force us to part. There is consolation in having her two daughters, Dolly and Lucy, to carry on in her memory in case I outlast my good little Dirty Face.

Some bovines are born gentle and dangerously — for their own good — friendly. Sweetie Pie is one. She was born in the corral, and immediately accepted human beings as a natural part of her world. Neighbor Pete had never seen a calf that would rub against his leg like a kitten until she began to slip up and nuzzle him as he was milking Dirty Face. At this time, she is a yearling and has been out on the range for months. But when you come upon her, she will let you walk right up and scratch her head as if she were a pet dog. This is something of a worry. Some fellow looking for free meat wouldn't have any trouble catching her.

Yes, a cow-and-calf outfit, if you get close to it, involves taking care of *individuals,* in sickness or in health, for better or for worse, until death do you part. The slogan "There's nothing to do with a cow but eat her" is a Madison-Avenue quip which has meaning if you live in an air-conditioned glass-and-concrete fully-applianced wholly-artificial environment that shields you from the dirt and sweat and heart strain and sweet satisfaction of living in the cow country. But hear me. Get down to earth and become acquainted with a good old cow, and if, in the end, somebody has to eat her, *it ain't going to be you.*

Given a chance, most old cowpunchers stay with the cattle beyond their capacities to endure the hardships involved. It isn't only that they love the freedom of the back country. They like cows. I met an ex-cowboy at the auction not long ago. "I come down here," he said, grinning self-consciously, "to pick up a few droppings. It's as close as I can come to an old cow any more."

Western lore will be forever popular because of the sweep of scenic wild country; the exciting power and rhythm of galloping horses; and the picturesque, strangely-touching beauty of the "thundering herds" — even if in real life they are gentle and you have to push them along. All the decor and landscaping money can buy cannot arouse the quick inspiriting delight of driving a bunch of your own cattle along the rugged trails of mountain and canyon country — especially if they are whitefaces and fat, and have their calves along to bawl at. It is fun to work cattle and to have cows to take care of.

Where the cows are, there is peace and quiet and room to ride in. Never mind wishing for physical comfort: not in the arid Southwest where cow people repeatedly bear terrific hardships for the sake of keeping their cattle alive and functioning. Or for the arrogant peace that means relief from financial worry. A special peace, a kind of happy restfulness, abides in the land of the cow. The naturalist John Burroughs said: "I had rather have the care of cattle than be the keeper of the great seal of the nation. Where the cow is, there is Arcadia; so far as her influence prevails, there is contentment, humility, and the sweet homely life."

I imagine that Mr. Burroughs had in mind the small lush meadows of a rain-favored country dotted here and there with "The-friendly-cow-all-red-and-white-I-love-with-all-my-heart;-She-gives-me-cream-with-all-her-might-To-eat-with-apple-tart." But even in the wilderness, to live close to cows is a special pleasure hard to renounce once you've had it. You have what city folks think they long for: room to relax in.

You are out in the cool promising dawn, sweet with honeysuckle fragrance. As far as the eye can see or the ear can hear, you are the only specimen of the worry-wart species. You can forget how you look and what people will say, and enjoy what is at hand. You turn the hose on the roses and wonder at their colors and texture. As the sun strikes the treetops, you see the brilliant shimmer of that wonderful green that is the plant's payment on the precious water you have advanced. A quail across the gullies calls to his gang that it is about time to rally for the raid on the chicken scratch that falls like manna shortly after daylight. From a high tree, a cardinal's whistle challenges you and your cats and the whole world. From over on the west ridge, bright with the yellow blossoms of the May palo verdes, a cow stops picking at the spiny cactus and cries out to her calf: "Come on, let's go over to the corral and see if the *vieja* will hand us out some green alfalfa hay."

Before the sun blazes forth in its glory from the empty sky, you stop to take an appraising look all around at the everlasting hills and stony ridges, and are immediately impressed by their determination to have a green covering (or a faded facsimile thereof) — a determination so inherently strong that only man's excavations and costly asphalt and cement can conquer it. In wonder, you sigh with pleasure at sight of the battalions of desert mesquite, most

bountiful of all trees, that seem to be lined up in battle
array against the famine that plagues the creatures of this
Land of Little Rain as they defy the drying sun and the
long drought by putting on green gowns sprigged with the
golden plumes that will mature into nourishing *péchitas*
for the hungry animals.

It is heartening to get out in the best hour of the day —
it *is* the best hour for every kind of activity, even sleep-
ing! — and glimpse the beauty and goodness of the wide
space you occupy alone. Then you go around to fix up the
clothes line the pesky horse has broken down. A sliver
from an old pole slides in under your fingernail. While
you're trying to work it out with your pocketknife, a gnat
dives into your eye. Oh, well . . . . . .

Eighty years or so ago, the cow country was a far-off
frontier to which prosperous eastern parents could send
their problem sons as remittance men. Thirty or forty
years ago, mother and father came west, too, sparking the
heyday of the dude ranches. Now the whole family, ever
more prosperous, has come out to buy the country and
make it over. All kinds of people want a cattle ranch.

When I lived in Tucson as a primary teacher, it was a
live-and-let-live cowtown, and a railroad division point
where you could walk down the main street any Saturday
afternoon and meet many of your friends and acquaint-
ances. There was leisure and space, and if you needed a
wilderness, it was close at hand. Now there is boom and
industrialization — and a terrific longing for the wide
open country. Most people you meet think they'd like to
have a ranch. Actually, what they want is a home in the
country with an income to keep it up. A modern home.
In a safe country. They want the joys of the wilds, but
know nothing of its terrors and hardships. They long for
a good horse in the crisp dawn; a lowing herd in the sun-

bright noon; a fragrant garden in the quiet twilight — before they go indoors to their push-button gadgets.

I am pretty far out, but Progress will catch up some day. When I am bumbling around in a wheelchair, a sharp real estate salesman will drive up to offer to buy and sell my outfit. Not for cash, of course. Who would want to give an old woman cash? How about trading for peace and comfort in some nice clean house in town with a porch and a rocking chair?

"Young Lady," he'll say (that's what you get called when it no longer applies) "you can't make it here any longer. Your fences are down. Your corrals are falling to staves. Your pipeline has rusted away. Your trees are dying for lack of care. Your house is too much for you. You can not cope with a place so large. I'd like to see you resting easy. You could have a little house in town and be comfortable. No hard work to do. No insoluble worries. Let me have your little ranch for my client and you . . ."

"Just a minute," I'll interrupt. "This nice quiet home you want me to trade for. Is it located where I can hear a cow bawl?"

"Oh, no. It's near the doctors and the hospital and . . ."

That's the moment I'll lower my ear trumpet and sic the dogs on him.